MW00681730

The Measure of
a Man is the Size
of His Toolbox

The Measure of a Man is the Size of His Toolbox

CAROL PICARD

Mosaic Press
Oakville, ON. - Buffalo, N.Y.

Canadian Cataloguing in Publication Data

Picard, Carol, 1957-
    The measure of a man is the size of his toolbox

ISBN 0-88962-599-9

1. Canadian wit and humor (English).*   I.Title

PS8581.I37M4 1995   C818'.5402   C95-932715-0
PR9199.3.P53M4 1995

Published by MOSAIC PRESS, P.O. Box 1032, Oakville, Ontario, L6J
5E9, Canada. Offices and warehouse at 1252 Speers Road, Units #1&2,
Oakville, Ontario, L6L 5N9, Canada and Mosaic Press, 85 River Rock
Drive, Suite 202, Buffalo, N.Y., 14207, USA.

Mosaic Press acknowledges the assistance of the Canada Council, the
Ontario Arts Council, the Ontario Ministry of Culture, Tourism and
Recreation and the Dept. of Canadian Heritage, Government of Canada,
for their support of our publishing programme.

Cover Illustration by John G. Burke
Book design by Susan Parker
Printed and bound in Canada
ISBN   0-88962-599-9

In Canada:
MOSAIC PRESS, 1252 Speers Road, Units #1&2, Oakville, Ontario,
L6L 5N9, Canada. P.O. Box 1032, Oakville, Ontario, L6J 5E9
In the United States:
MOSAIC PRESS, 85 River Rock Drive, Suite 202, Buffalo, N.Y., 14207
In the UK and Western Europe:
DRAKE INTERNATIONAL SERVICES, Market House, Market Place,
Deddington, Oxford. OX15 OSF

PREFACE

Four years ago, in what can only be called serendipity, I ended up in a little slice of paradise nestled in the heart of the Canadian Rockies, just outside the Banff National Park. The mountains are majestic, the water pristine and the air so clean you can smell it. At last count, there were about 7,000 trusty souls who are proud to call themselves Canmorons. and that hammering sound we awaken to each morning is the frenzied pace of residential construction to accommodate more and more newcomers who want to share the dream.

As part of my job as editor of the weekly *Canmore Leader*, I am required each week to write precisely 3,024 characters on my trusty Mac to fill an op-ed space that was probably, in its concept, intended to be home to a thoughtful, reasoned discourse on development, tourism, the environment, religion, politics or philosophy in general.

Unfortunately, the job came without an instruction manual, and believing fervently that there is far too much weighty discourse going on in the world today, I opted for a somewhat more frivolous approach.

You will find no startling insight herein, no sagacious wisdom, no penetrating perspectives. Instead, you would be wise to put this book in the bathroom as soon as you buy it. It's that kind of a book. And no, this is not what I aspired to be when I grew up.

My thanks to Howard Aster at Mosaic Press for nurturing this little project and my publishers at WestMount Press, owners of the truly wonderful *Canmore Leader*, who have given me almost free reign to fill those 12 column inches with whatever I saw fit.

Mostly, thanks go to the people of Canmore, who are among the best neighbors I've ever had the privilege of knowing and who collectively make this such a special place to live.

Carol Picard

TABLE OF CONTENTS

SECTION ONE
PARADISE TEMPORARILY MISPLACED

LEARNING LIFE'S BIG
LESSONS IN A SMALL TOWN

September 1, 1992

Happy Anniversary to me. Today it's been one whole year since I moved to town and shackled my leg to a desk at the *Canmore Leader*.

When I first came to Canmore, I was under the impression that this would be the proverbial cushy job. Sleepy little newspaper in mountain community seeks reporter to work for little money in the heart of the world's best ski resorts and hiking trails. Apply to Larry Marshall.

I skied two days last winter, and the only hike I've thus far taken was a mad dash up Yamnuska trying to get a photo of an injured climber being rescued by helicopter. I've yet to see Grotto Canyon, Grassi Lakes or the Heart Creek Trail. My fishing rod is dusty and my mountain bike's still for sale in the window of Spoke 'N Edge.

Marshall made me promise to stay a year, tired as he was of the revolving door of reporters departing in three months for greener pastures.

I've learned a lot this year. I still haven't mastered the concept of time management, and I still haven't learned to Just Say No to the six-day work week, but what the heck. You have to leave something to learn for another day.

I've learned that not all small towns are boring, small-minded enclaves of humdrum existence. I've learned that small town does not mean small issues. This past year in Canmore has immersed me in a microcosm of the issues facing the world in general. Green dollars vs. green space. How many other reporters get to live an issue of such magnitude so intimately?

I've learned to no longer judge a person by their clothes, because in this town the better dressed person is usually a real estate salesman, while the bearded guy in the jeans and windbreaker is the Ph.D.

I've learned to love the Planning Act, the Municipal Government Act and the Land Use Bylaws. Upon them our orderly existence depends.

I've learned to appreciate Indian Time, a clockless concept borrowed from our friends up the road in Morley and entirely applicable to life in Canmore, where things do usually start on time but don't officially get underway for 20 minutes while everyone catches up on what everyone else has been doing since last they met. Even Council generally gets a 15-minute grace period, even though they don't usually want to know what the others have been up to.

I've learned what accountability is, a truly interesting lesson. Never before have I had to stand in line at the grocery store behind the businessman who was the subject of this week's front page story. Never before have I had private citizens and elected officials slam the phone down in my ear and felt it so keenly. Everyone is my neighbor. I've tried to learn diplomacy and I've tried to learn when to keep my mouth shut. And when hanging up first just makes good sense.

I've learned that some of those same elected officials are among the most wonderful and intelligent people I've ever met. So are their critics. I've shared bar stools with both. Every issue has two sides, and there is truth in both. Usually I find myself firmly entrenched on one side. Sometimes I find myself in the middle. Sometimes I find myself on both sides. Sometimes I can't see what all the fuss is about, but somewhere, someone in this town cares deeply.

So here it is, a year later. Another year older and deeper in debt. As you read this, I am somewhere else, lying on a sunny beach reading trashy detective novels. My year of indentured servitude is over, Marshall. I've kept up my part of the bargain.

But I'll be back tomorrow. I wouldn't miss it for the world.

Only in Canmore you say? Where else?

March 8, 1994

One of the most common descriptions you will ever hear about Canmore is that we are a unique community. We're special, without really knowing why.

I mean, here we are, an otherwise motley collection of individuals who have all migrated to the mountains so we can ski and hike at leisure and then we take on 90-hour-a-week jobs so we can survive in this hyperactive real estate market, and we consider ourselves lucky.

We're special, all right.

Other communities claim uniqueness by building giant papier mache Ukrainian Easter eggs or alien spacecraft landing pads that loom over the prairie landscape, beckoning travellers to stop and see what the heck is going on. Mother Nature took care of our need for looming edifices, so we satisfy our instinctive need for construction in other ways.

We build houses. Lots and lots of houses, so that when those highway travellers, who've left their cars to ogle the towering granite, utter what is *always* the standard opening line for a newcomer to Canmore -- "What are housing prices like around here, anyway?" -- we have a variety of options for them to choose from. We're special because we've been conditioned to believe affordable housing starts at $160,000.

We're special because we live in a town in which politicians would rather quit than fight and the most popular fundraising activity is the public shaving of one's head; where it rains in February and snows in July and every vehicle carries an emergency winter survival kit in the dead of summer; where the skirl of bagpipes is more likely to be heard on a summer morning than the roar of a lawnmower -- unless you live within the confines of those instant neighborhoods north of the TransCanada Highway, in which case you are awakened every Saturday morning by the whine of buzz saws and Makita power drills.

We live in a town where hotels list themselves in the phone book under T for "The "

In Canmore the most popular items for interior decoration are either antlers, stuffed moose heads or exquisite, painted mountain views that mirror exactly the scene out the living room window. The most popular modes of transportation are either knobby-wheeled bicycles that cost more than a Honda or little neon green canvas trailers, in which we place our infants so we can drag them around behind the knobby tires.

In Canmore, careless elk are the biggest road hazard and traffic on one of the busiest routes out of town is more likely to be held up by salt-starved bighorn sheep licking the highway than rock slides or blizzards.

In Canmore, people wear sandals year round, eliminating the wardrobe indicator people the world over take as the first sign of spring. Here, the first sign of spring is when people put shorts on under their parkas.

In Canmore we make accommodations for our lack of ocean front property by letting our potholes grow to such a size that the water therein is affected by the twice daily pull of the lunar cycle.

MIGHTY OAKS FROM TINY ACORNS GROW

May 10, 1994

Every once in a while I find myself bemused by the varied paths on which people travel to Canmore. How the heck did such a disparate collection of souls all wind up in the same place, anyway?

Some came, and still come, for emotional and spiritual reasons, a need to be surrounded by majestic mountains and nature's serenity.

Others came, and still come, for profit or livelihood. Many come for all of the above.

I'm not talking about Canmore's earliest days, when Europeans and Asians emigrated from distant continents to toil in the bowels of the coal mines. Their names survive in this town because their descendants made a decision, conscious or otherwise, not to move.

It's the rest of us Canmorons I find myself dwelling on, we who had to start from somewhere else. It is these people's stories I never tire of hearing, and in Canmore it seems everybody has one.

Twenty years ago scores of Twentysomethings showed up here looking for their own personal version of Walden Puddle. Some were seeking the proverbial good vibrations. Some were avoiding a war in southeast Asia. Some just ran out of money as they hitchhiked west and found an amenable bunch of people with whom to hang out.

I believe all of this because of the enormous number of people who, in response to the question, will say they came here to ski for three months in 1976 and haven't left since.

In keeping with the fashion of the day, they had long hair and unkempt beards and baggy jeans. They skied as often as possible and those without gainful employment coined the phrase "UIC Ski Team". Others took to climbing the faces of the mountains, while still others took up painting, hiking, cycling, canoeing, kayaking and parasailing, as soon as the latter was invented.

Many took manual laboring jobs as carpenters and truckers, anything that would allow them to stay in this little piece of paradise, feed the children that somehow came to be and still ski and climb as they often as they wanted.

The town fathers in those days probably looked somewhat askance at these newcomers and harrumphed a bit about how the town sure was changing, but I've heard some absolutely wonderful stories about the generosity and kindness those "oldtimers" showed the "newcomers", particularly when the new kids on the block started having their babies and settling into their new $3,000 homes.

These days, those "newcomers" are the middle aged and middle class establishment in Canmore. Their kids are in high school, they have jobs and mortgages, and many own their own contracting and construction firms. They sit on the Planning Commission and the Hospital Board and the Development Appeal Board and even Council. They teach in the schools and nurse in the hospital and own their own restaurants.

I think of all this every time I pass one of the new Twentysomethings on the street, and I try to look beyond the shaved head and triple-pierced nose and baggy jeans. I try not to judge when I overhear his or her glee at having gone snowboarding for 31 consecutive days in March.

I harbor no ill will at the carefree existence and seemingly aimless direction of their lives. This could be the person we elect as Mayor in 2014.

IT'S ONLY BAD WHEN SOMEONE GETS HURT

April 28, 1992

The assignment: put on your best dress and a pair of high heels that haven't been used in so long they need to be dusted, go to a party where there's a built-in shortage of men with whom to dance and then, when you snag one, *pay* him for the privilege.

A dirty job, but someone had to do it. An in-depth investigation into the political incorrectness and reverse sexism of *Puttin' on the Ritz*, the largest fundraising event on the Canmore social calendar.

Scandal beckoned. Other reporters uncover illicit arms sales to Iran and sexual infidelities of presidential candidates. So okay, this isn't quite on that scale, but hey, I wanted the exciting life of a small town journalist.

I went incognito, in the aforementioned high heels and party frock. Everyone else was in disguise, too. I barely recognized a soul.

I must confess, I approached the assignment with some trepidation. Take 200 women who want to play dress up, put them in a room with 50 good looking guys in tuxedos whose sole purpose is to wait on the women hand and foot and dance with them on demand and the potential is there for some serious craziness.

Because I'm a thorough kind of person, my investigation wasn't complete until about 3:30 a.m. Of craziness there was plenty. I shot several rolls of film. The negatives can be purchased, for a price.

I asked several of the men if they felt compromised. Indeed they did, they grinned.

One allowed as how he'd "rather dance with 200 women than sell cookies at a bake sale." Hmm. A dad at a bake sale. Another story for another day.

Here's our MLA in the kitchen, wearing sneakers with his tux, for Pete's sake, serving up chicken breasts. Are MLAs supposed to do this kind of thing? Is this what we elected him for? And a certain tall town councillor in a red smoking jacket, if you please, dancing up a storm with anyone who had the price of a ticket. How am I supposed to take these guys seriously now?

(How are they supposed to take *me* seriously after I've stuffed dance tickets in their pockets? Have I been irrevocably compromised? The next time I have to ask either of them the tough questions, will I be overwhelmed by the shameful memory of having paid for their services? Or empowered at the knowledge that they can be bought?)

It *was* pretty politically incorrect, especially for 1992. It was also a lot of fun, and a lot of money did get raised for the day care. Besides, political correctness is a rather disturbing concept when a vocal majority can dictate what they deem to be appropriate thought and behavior on all. I think it's healthy to indulge in a little political incorrectness now and then.

And the sexism, of course, was rampant.

But you know what? No one cared. A good time was had by all, nearly $7,000 got raised for new toys and carpet and paint and no one got hurt.

Except for 50 guys whose feet probably hurt like the dickens on Sunday.

How to tell you're here and not there

September 8, 1992

Every Monday I go to Banff. It's a necessary evil. For reasons still unknown to me, our production facilities and presses are up the road in the high-rent district of the Bow Valley.

I don't like going to Banff. You'll note I'm not saying I don't *like* Banff, I just don't like *going* there. After a year of bucolic sedateness in Canmore, I cringe at the urban pace assumed by Alberta's Official Mountain Paradise. I imagine people from Exshaw must feel the same way coming to Canmore. Or the folks from Seebe when they enter the corporate limits of Exshaw.

It's purely a personal thing. I mean, there's nothing inherently *wrong* with the place, it's just that it's, well, it's so *citified*. (Note again, please, I did not say civilized, I said citified. There's a difference.)

On Banff Avenue cars slow to a snail-like crawl while drivers negotiate bulldozers, ripped up pavement, tour buses and tourists who think they're going to find an unused, RV-sized parking spot. Then there's those of the pedestrian variety who wander into traffic with necks craned, searching for the mountain peaks it's rumored you can see from downtown.

In Canmore, all cars have to slow to a snail-like crawl on Main Street while drivers manoeuvre with one hand, freeing the other to wave and honk at passing pedestrians and oncoming traffic because you must greet everyone you know lest you never again be invited to another backyard barbecue.

In Banff, summer road construction is a way of life, an indication of the change of seasons as certain as the first avalanche of spring. In Canmore, road construction is newsworthy. We take pictures of it for the paper.

Banff has traffic lights. Canmore has stop signs that mean: "Slow down to a moderate roll." These do not apply to cyclists.

In Banff, the tourists wear shorts and the locals wear business suits to work.

In Canmore, the only people who wear business suits are from out of town and they're here to buy a house. Or build a hotel.

In Banff, you can get take-out food from nearly every nation in the world *and* Teenburgers and Big Macs.

In Canmore, we're still griping about the Boston Pizza and there's a petition making the rounds because there's a Dairy Queen rumored for the highway.

Banff has a year-round population of occasionally-hostile elk to annoy the locals and amuse the tourists. We have ducks and bunnies.

In Canmore you can still buy a T-shirt that doesn't have the name of the town on it or Canada's flag emblazoned across the chest. In Banff you can't, but you *can* buy Callebaut chocolate and fresh ramen noodles.

In Banff people line up to get into the bars and restaurants on a Saturday night. We don't line up, except of course in the grocery store, where it's mandatory to move as slowly as possible so as to catch up on any gossip one didn't read on the bulletin boards and telephone poles around town.

People who live in Banff know what they are. They are Banffites, plain and simple. We in Canmore still don't really know what our correct appellation is -- Canmorite or Canmoron -- except for 16 per cent of our population, who are Calgarians.

A LETTER FROM THE EDITOR

February 11, 1992

Dear Readers:

There's trouble in River City, folks. War has broken out. Unstated, undeclared, unnoticed by most, but war nonetheless -- the War of the Guest Speakers.

We have no idea when exactly it started. It sort of seeped into town like smoke from a smoldering Three Sisters' scrub pile. We three ink-stained and increasingly sleepless wretches here at the *Leader* share a scant 18 months' experience in this town, so none of us were actually around to witness the first literary SCUD, but near as we can tell it came from BowCORD, the Bow Corridor Organization for Responsible Development.

(We like acronyms. We'd much rather write something like TASS or PRAVDA than have to keep writing "the group" or "the organization" or "that bunch of people who all sit on the same side of an issue".)

BowCORD seems to have fired the first missive by providing a steady stream of letters to this paper, much to the delight of a certain recently transplanted editor who was beginning to think he'd have to start resorting to the imaginary citizens used by many a weekly newspaper editor in the absence of real local issues. Nope, these were actual, honest-to-God Concerned Citizens.

But soon, along came another group of equally Concerned Citizens, and they called themselves PROD -- People for Responsible and Orderly Decision-making.

Now, at first glance, one might assume these folks are somewhat similar because they both have the word "responsible" in their titles, but they're kind of on opposite sides. It's all in how you say it. One's for RESPONSIBLE development, the other for responsible DEVELOPMENT. Oops, make that decision-making.

Anyway, the only issue on which these two groups seem to see eye to eye is the "let's make those dumb *Leader* reporters abandon any semblance of a normal life they ever had" issue.

Lots of stories about these groups of Concerned Citizens appeared in the newspaper, and even more letters to the editor. Then they began bringing in The Guest Speakers.

BowCORD had the first meeting. Then the Chamber of Commerce had a meeting, to refute what BowCORD's speaker had said. Two days later a BowCORD member gave a speech in Calgary about development in Canmore. Five days later the Chamber of Commerce had another meeting, to which we were cordially invited to hear Canmore Alpine Development Company President Hal Walker speak. PROD got in on the act four days later, with a meeting to which they invited Three Sisters Resorts' President Richard Melchin.

Three days later it was BowCORD's turn to have a meeting. A three-day lull followed, and then it was the Chamber's turn again. Only two days elapsed before BowCORD got MLA Brian Evans to host a tea at the Bow Valley Senior's Lodge. Unless PROD or the Chamber jumps into the picture, there's a two week hiatus before BowCORD's open house on Feb. 27. But the very next day, the Chamber's invited Wild Rose MP Louise Feltham to speak at a luncheon meeting. And just for good measure, they're throwing in Environment Minister Ralph Klein to speak on March 13.

It's starting to feel like a high stakes poker game. We'll see your Evans and raise you a Klein. And just like a really good poker game, there's a few people around the table who aren't getting *nearly* enough sleep.

Carol Picard
(Not Dear Sir)

Unsettled and Intermittent is
a Normal State for Us

Now that Easter has come and gone, people the world over
know that it's officially appropriate to wear white shoes once
more.

Of course, in Canmore these days white footwear usually
means Sorel boots, but at least we're in the right end of the
color chart.

Springtime in the Rockies is such a difficult time of year
for those of us who still need help dressing in the morning.
When you have to turn on the weather channel and consult
the national meteorologists to figure out what is appropriate
attire for the day, you know you're a pretty hopeless case.

Looking out the window before leaving the house is of
no help. When the sun is shining on Fifth Street, it could be
snowing on Main Street and raining in Cougar Creek. Or it
could be sunny and snowing at the same time in the same place.
Occasionally we are treated to sun, snow and rain simultaneously,
leaving one hemming and hawing when out of town relatives
call to make idle conversation.

"How's the weather out there?" they will ask.

"Well, it's intermittent," you will reply.

"Intermittent what?"

"Intermittent everything."

Even the precipitation seems confused these days,
unsure of whether it wants to be snowflakes or raindrops.

Studying one's neighbors for clues as to what we should
wear seems rather pointless, judging by those around us. We
are all confused at the moment.

There are those who dress in layers -- rainproof, down-
filled outerwear worn over shorts worn over long johns -- and
somehow manage to combine every piece of clothing in their
closets into one all-purpose, all-season wardrobe.

Then there are those who dress for a particular season
and pray that the weather that day will come close. In the same

restaurant on the same day you will find people dressed as though they are going to spend a day at the beach, sitting next to those outfitted for a polar expedition. And like a stopped watch that is right twice daily, spring weather in the Rockies means both of these people are probably wearing the appropriate clothes for at least part of the day.

Toques and straw bonnets share hooks on the wall. Boots and sandals vie for space in the closet. The parkas are kept as handy as the umbrellas, the snow shovel and the rake lean side by side against the garage.

Picking an activity for an idle day in April is as fraught with uncertainty as picking a jacket. Our urban brethren show up in town with both mountain bikes and skis strapped to the roof racks, scanning the skies with the same look of perplexity that we Canmorites adopt around the middle of March and maintain until the end of May. (In a good year, of course. We have been known to golf in blizzards in August and get good swimming weather in January. If the unsettled weather only lasts for three months, we are fortunate indeed.)

TRYING TO SECOND GUESS
THE NEWSMAKERS

December 28, 1993

Another Christmas passed, another Christmas stocking *sans* crystal ball. That's it. That's the last letter from me old Santa Claus is getting.

I really wanted one this year. Actually, I desperately needed one. Heck, I'd have settled for a Ouija board, some tarot cards, a divining rod, *anything* that would help me predict and second guess the fickle vagaries of news as we know it in this town.

Just once I'd like to know what's in those little packets Council gets, the ones stamped Not For Press Or Public, so that when we report a story we've got *all* the information instead of just that which *someone* deems is all we need.

Just once I'd like to know what *really* goes on in provincial cabinet meetings, when they're making arrangements to dispose of that enormous portion of my paycheque which I earn and they spend. Just once I'd like to know

Oh, what the heck. Skip the crystal ball. I'll just throw caution to the wind and hazard a few predictions of what *I* think the next 12 months will see here in Canmore.

1. Council will call a by-election to fill Councillor Ross Larsen's seat. Many people will enter the race and find themselves the centre of attention wherever they go for the duration of the campaign. When it is over, no one will admit to being happy with the outcome and our new Councillors will then enter that select club of those who know one of life's more obscure truths: Running for public office is good for your social life. Winning is not.

2. Canmore will not be chosen as the site of the new NAFTA Environmental Secretariat. It will, however, be awarded a consolation prize. It will be selected for the new 1,359-unit medium security Clayquot Correctional Centre for those convicted of demonstrating the strength of their convictions.

3. Dog and cat owners in Canmore will rise up in arms once the true implications of the new Animal Control Bylaw are understood and appreciated. They will write Letters to the Editor and protest to Council, and some of them may even join the ranks of the felonious tree-huggers for daring to ride their bicycles with an unleashed dog by their side.

4. Twenty gazillion houses, 39 hotels and 14 new restaurants will be built. Concerned taxpayers will write Letters to the Editor and protest to Council. Council will listen with sympathy and understanding and try to explain that we are in a free market economy and we can't stop progress.

5. It will rain on at least one of the two days of the Heritage Folk Festival.

6. Ralph Klein will kiss and make up with Mike Harcourt before announcing that anyone who has ever

visited an emergency ward, attended school or sneezed in public in Alberta must now fork over a retroactive $1,000 for the added cost this imposed on our deficit. He will then depart for his $3,000 one-week fishing vacation in B.C.
7. Another 2,000 babies will be born in Canmore this year, paving the way for new controversy in about five years when a new school will be needed and no one will be able to figure out why.
8. There will be rampant rumors racing through town about graft, greed, corruption and deception practised by Calgary developers, school board trustees and provincial politicians.
9. Liquor prices will go up. Count on it.

WE'RE OLDER AND RICHER,
BUT ARE WE ANY WISER?

August 23, 1994

It finally happened.

I left town for two weeks and no one built a new hotel, restaurant, golf course, parkade or monolith in my absence. Imagine my surprise when I returned and found things just as I left them.

Every once in a while you've just got to leave paradise to appreciate it. Absence, however brief, brings a new clarity to one's vision. All this week I have been struck by the signs of how Canmore is changing.

Evidently someone snuck in overnight and left a Jag in every driveway. Our streets are now increasingly clogged with Mercedes, Jeeps, a whole heap of Beemers and a bumper crop of restored ragtop sports cars of British extraction, some of which are driven by men of an advanced level of age, financial security and personal insecurity, judging by the babes sharing the leather upholstery with them.

Those who drive these ostentatious displays of disposable income are at least partially responsible for Sign of Change Number Two. The traffic jam at the four-way stop on Main Street and Seventh Avenue now approximates on a Wednesday morning what it once was on a Saturday afternoon on a long weekend in August. Anyone who doubts our rapid growth rate need only stand on the balcony here at the *Canmore Leader* for half an hour to be convinced. When all the Jags, Beemers and Benz's get backed up at the intersection, Canmore bears a distinct resemblance to Vail, Colorado, without Cher.

Where there's money, there's those who feel no compunction to earn it themselves. Crime appears to be on the increase, as evidenced by the marathon police report this week. Bikes, especially those of the unlocked variety, still seem to be the favorite booty. However, instead of lifting the garden variety $250 wheels, thieves are now finding themselves the proud new fencers of the $1,500 titanium framed luxury models.

The infusion of wealth to this community has given rise to Sign of Change Number Four. The biggest growth industry in Canmore is no longer construction, real estate sales or private childbirth classes. It is financial management consulting and planning services. Trust me on this.

In the past month, I have had 64 offers of free newspaper columns from firms whose sole purpose is to help you park your extra cashburgers in high yield mutual funds, stocks, bonds and seasonally adjusted RRSPs with fluctuating interest rates tied to daily news reports out of Quebec.

I may have to take these people up on their offers. Goodness knows, we could all use a little free financial advice. Like, where does it come from and how can I get some?

Which came first, the Jags or the money managers? I have no idea. I do know that we are, on the surface, seeing a huge increase in older and affluent in this town, and once more I am completely out of step with the rest of the community.

Except the older part.

THE TOURIST AS A
SOCIOLOGICAL SUB-SPECIES

June 7, 1992

Tourist Season is upon us, a time when people flee the familiar comforts of house and home and manicured lawn and go somewhere else to see how other people live, while those other people go somewhere else to see how other people, who have also gone somewhere else, live.

Unless, of course, you're a Canmoron, in which case you flee deep into the backcountry to get away from the RVs cruising Main Street for a parking space.

"Hey Martha! Sign says they got a golf course. Wonder what housing prices are like around here "

Consider for a moment, if you will, the lowly tourist. Not the guy who sails off into the Caribbean on a Windjammer, or even the tourist who throws his clubs in the car for a week at Peter's Playground, but the poor working stiff who scrapes together enough cash once a year to feed the gas-guzzling mobile motel room in which he and his family will spend two weeks dining on egg sandwiches and looking at things they don't have back home go flashing past the windows. Kind of like TV without the remote.

Recently it has come to my attention, thanks to an anonymous local contributor who is under the mistaken impression that I actually have time for discretionary reading, that tourism is being studied in some circles as a sociological entity. Like chimps in a cage, the tourist is figuratively dissected as a species unto itself with such observations as: "Tourism is a form of play which, like all play, has profound roots in reality, but for the success of which a great deal of make-believe is necessary." (Erik Cohen: Authenticity and Commoditization in Tourism, Annals of Tourism Research.)

Gee. All this time, while you though you were having fun (or just getting away and being miserable in unfamiliar surroundings) you were just fooling yourself into *thinking* you were having fun.

Ponder this little gem: "Given the present sociohistorical epoch, it is not a surprise to find that tourists believe sightseeing is a leisure activity and fun, even when it requires more effort and organization than many jobs." (Dean MacCannell; Arrangements of Social Space in Tourist Settings, American Journal of Sociology.)

And ain't that the truth. I've done the RV vacation, and I can attest to the amount of effort it takes to transport all of your creature comforts around the country in the belly of a steel whale.

I've done the camping thing, too. And the golfing thing, and the fishing thing, and even the Disneyworld thing. I think this year it's time to stay behind in this Future Destination Resort and watch the tourists search for parking.

With luck I'll get two weeks, before the snow flies again, to sling a hammock in the backyard and reread *my* favorite student of tourists and tourism, award-winning *Miami Herald* reporter Carl Hiassen.

"It's a tourist trap, plain and simple. It brings traffic, garbage, litter, air pollution, effluent -- Kingsbury cares nothing about preserving the habitat. He's a developer." (Carl Hiassen; *Native Tongue*.)

Hiassen's books, I believe, have been banned in Florida.

How do you put a
price tag on sunshine?

July 19, 1994

A developer has stolen my sunshine.

He didn't mean to, I'm sure. He was just doing his job. But one day it was there, and the next day it wasn't.

The small house to which we moved in April was once situated beside a tiny, dilapidated bungalow. The view from our huge kitchen window was, if not pristine, at least inoffensive, and the sunlight that poured through that window flooded the kitchen from early morning until late afternoon, making it the warmest, cheeriest room in the house. My houseplants thrived, both there and on the second floor landing whose window faced the same direction.

The shack, alas, was sold and a brand new, two-storey four-plex is being erected on the lot. Where once I gazed on weeds and an overchoked garden, I now have a plywood wall a scant 10 feet from my window. Not a single sunbeam gets through. My kitchen is dark and chilly, my second floor the same. Soon, once the new neighbors have moved in, we will have to draw the blinds permanently to preserve any semblance of privacy.

The developer who constructed this edifice is a very nice man, making his living with small scale projects such as this. No golf course, no 800-room hotel. Just a nice little four-plex of condominiums. The land was zoned for multi-family, he bought it fair and square and is exercising his right to earn a living.

Since this project began at least a dozen men have been employed full time, hammering and pounding and plumbing and wiring and politely waiting until at least 8 a.m. before switching on the power tools.

Were it not for this developer and this project, I wonder what they would otherwise have done this summer.

The downtown residential area is almost entirely zoned for increased densities, and this newspaper has more than once editorialized about the wisdom of that decision. Far better to put more people in smaller units in this area than to allow construction of 2,500 square foot monstrosities up the sides of the mountains.

But it's easy to editorialize about a concept. My sunshine has been stolen and I'm not sure I like it happening in my own backyard.

The effects of growth and development are as evident as the spreading expanse of rooftops in Cougar Creek and the growing crowds on downtown streets, but they're also as intangible as the loss of enjoyment one gets from drinking your morning coffee at a sun-drenched table. How can you put a price tag on sunshine?

From the tiny back window in the kitchen, I have a narrow but unobstructed view of Chinaman's Peak. My sight line, however, crosses a tiny shack diagonal to our home, a house that will no doubt be torn down and a four- or eight-plex built in its place sometime in the near future. In the other direction, I have a view of just the peaks of the Three Sisters. A four-plex across the lane blocks out the rest. This, then, is progress.

When I go for walks throughout my neighborhood, I always notice the other tiny houses. In those long-gone days, they opted for smaller dwellings and larger yards in which their children had space to play. These yards are increasingly scarce commodities in my neighborhood these days.

Sometimes, people with whom I'm strolling play a kind of guessing game, wondering aloud what the property is worth and when they're selling. Me, I secretly pray that they'll hang on for as long as they can.

BEFORE WE GET TOO BIG
FOR OUR BRIDGES

July 5, 1994

Another wonderful Canada Day has come and gone, another summer long weekend spent studying the faces of the Main Street throng and wondering -- when did Canmore get so big?

It didn't, of course, get *so* big. It's getting bigger, to be sure, and before long we'll see 20,000 people lining Main Street instead of 5,000, but thus far, before the results of our latest census are in, we are still officially small town.

It certainly must have seemed that way to the gazillion visitors we had last weekend. How many of them, I wonder, were urbanites from downstream? How many of them looked around at our increasingly congested streets and growing urban sprawl and sighed longingly for such a simple, quiet, uncomplicated way of life?

(How do they do it, Henry? There isn't even a Costco in this town. How do you think they survive?)

It's a big assumption, I know, but I assume that, given the option, most people would prefer to live in our beautiful little mountain community than in the heat re-fracting heart of the crime-ridden concrete jungle. Ask any realtor in town. This is why we are growing too big for our bridges.

So, before we lose it entirely, let's reflect a little on why living in a small town is so infinitely preferable to life in the big city.

First of all, there's the intimacy of small town life that means everyone knows you and what you are doing and with whom. To some this would seem claustrophobic, but from my perspective, it just keeps us honest.

Such intimacies mean the librarians get to know your reading tastes and remember you every time a book they think you'd like appears on the shelves. If you're a *really* good patron, they'll reserve it without even telling you. And if you're a really, *really* good patron, they'll let you take out more books even when you've got overdue fines and their computer is threatening to revoke your credit rating.

In a small town, if you're inclined to stop at a local tavern for the occasional pint after work, you quickly discover who favors which watering hole and know immedi-ately where to call when you need to find your favorite plumber after 5 p.m.

A lot of people from the city make immediate cost comparisons and conclude, rightly, that some things cost more here. But *we* know that about a quarter of every buck spent in some of these local stores is going to show up on the backs of Little League baseball players, midget hockey play-ers, as floats in the Canada Day parade, in a great day care centre and the local food bank.

We actually know all of those who don silly costumes and march in our parades. Except the Shriners, of course. We suspect they only put on their fake beards and foil brogues to march in other towns' parades because they wouldn't be caught dead doing it on their own streets.

We have the best sausages west of Winnipeg and south of Edmonton. We can still buy our meat in quantities that bear some relation to the size of our families, and it comes individually wrapped in brown butchers' paper. Thus far our merchants have resisted any inclination to remain open 24 hours a day, seven days a week. This means we have less opportunity to spend on impulse, and we know that nothing is so important that it can't wait until tomorrow.

And the best part of all about small town living? We only have to remember four digits of our phone numbers.

THE SECOND ANNUAL ONLY-HALF-RIGHT YEAR IN PREVIEW

December 27, 1994

Every year at this time I get to go back through a year's worth of *Canmore Leaders* and put together the Year in Review issue. Every year I am struck by how far this little community has progressed in a very short 12 months. In 1993 we were consumed with development issues, environmental issues and Three Sisters Resorts. In 1994, it was development issues, environmental issues, Three Sisters Resorts and government cutbacks. Boy, the more things change...

Last year at this time I rather rashly and publicly made some predictions, and in keeping with my usual track record, I was half right. Of course, that means I was *only* half wrong. It didn't rain during the folk festival and there was no revolt by dog owners, liquor consumers or local taxpayers --except for that little byelection.

Emboldened by such stunning success, I offer here to you now the second annual Year in Preview. Ladies and gentlemen, place your bets.

1. Local politics will be in an uproar for most of the year as we head towards the October municipal election. Half of the current Councillors will announce in January they are definitely not running, change their minds by July and be sitting firmly on the fence by October. The other half are already campaigning. Canmore voters, in their usual scientific fashion, will cast their ballots after carefully polling their neighbors to find out their preferences and voting accordingly.

2. The provincial government will pass the new Planning Act and promptly order Canmore to rezone Quarry Lake. Council will have to pass a new land use category -- Puddle Side Residential.

3. Biologists will announce that collaring elk and moose with radio transmitters is a totally useless exercise in trying to determine their future survival as a species. Instead, they will collar all backcountry skiers, hikers and former Canmorons leaving town in search of less crowded environs to determine *their* future survival.

4. Four more provincial Cabinet ministers will move to Canmore, allowing for the weekly caucus meetings to be held in the old ALCB building and paving the way for the government to sell the Legislature to Triple 5 corporation for their newest theme park -- Fantasyland II.

5. Someone will write a Letter to the Editor criticizing people who let their dogs poop downtown. Someone else will suggest we diaper the elk.

6. Students will move into the new high school in September and the school board will shortly thereafter be hit with a barrage of complaints from parents upset that the board skimped on such things as carpeting, window coverings and light fixtures.

7. Main Street will be made a one-way street, creating mass confusion among downtown drivers who will demand a traffic light on every corner.

8. The RCMP will hire a consultant to teach local cyclists what a stop sign is and how to use the brakes on their bikes.

9. It will be hot and sunny next summer and cold and snowy next winter, with a few chinooks around Christmas. Everyone will comment on how unusual the weather is.

Section two
XX + XY = ??

The Measure of a Man Is
The Size of His Toolbox

May 11, 1993

Many years ago a friend of mine asked his roommate for permission to move his toolbox into their shared kitchen. The roommate, no doubt envisioning the haphazard collection of screwdrivers and wrenches in the trunk of his own MGB, agreed without hesitation.

The next day their kitchen table disappeared and a bungalow-sized red metal cabinet with 403 drawers and an assortment of compartments capable of concealing major home appliances was in its place. My friend, soon after, moved out.

And I, as impartial observer, learned a valuable lesson that has stood me well in my lifelong quest to try in some small way to understand men. The lesson is as follows -- Never underestimate the relationship between a man and his toolbox. Nor should you try to understand it. It's just one of those guy things.

Every man has a toolbox. Even if he has no fixed address, he can usually claim ownership of at least one screwdriver, which admits him into that loosely-based brotherhood of fix-it kinda guys who don't have to ask "who's that?" when asked to fetch a Phillips.

You can tell a lot about a guy by the size of his toolbox. If you're really serious about him, you can use it as a barometer to determine the course of your life and future spending habits.

If it's real small and fits into the glove compartment of his car, chances are he can recite from memory the phone number of every plumber, furnace repairman, carpenter, electrician and mechanic in town. Don't marry him unless he makes at least $50,000 or has a marketable skill like income tax preparation or dentistry so he can barter with those who really *can* fix things, and have the tools to prove it.

Then there are the medium-sized toolboxes with barely used or badly abused tools. These are owned by guys who just *think* they know how and have convinced themselves that, by buying the appropriate implement, they are equipped to handle the job.

A slight variation on the old "I think therefore I am." -- "I have a power drill, therefore I can rewire the basement."

Don't marry this man unless he earns at least $65,000 in his day job because you *know* it's going to cost you double every time the tradesman has to fix your husband's screw ups before the job can actually be started properly.

If his toolbox occupies roughly the same amount of floor space as, say, a three-car garage, chances are he's a pretty handy kind of guy. But he does come with his own special set of problems.

Don't expect to see much of him during the hardware store's hours of operations, and don't be too offended when he talks about his new router in the same tone of voice he used to propose to you.

Guys like this are prone to getting into boasting contests with like-minded buddies about the size of their tape measures, and they harass every pregnant woman known to them to save baby food jars so they can neatly sort by size and color their collection of finishing nails.

These guys are either frustrated blue collars masquerading as desk jockeys, in which case you will always have more bookshelves than you know how to fill, or they are professional tradesmen and you now live in a 45,000 square foot mansion with a bathroom that won't be finished until 1997.

ERIC LINDROS AND THE
PRICE OF CHEERIOS

July 28, 1992

I've been watching a lot of sports lately. An awful lot of sports. Huge, unmanageable amounts of sports. More sports than it is healthy for any one human being to watch. (It has nothing to do with the Olympics. It comes from hanging around with someone who lives with a golf club in one hand and a TV remote control in the other.)

This is an area of life that for 35 years I've managed thus far to successfully avoid, save for a brief and mercifully-ended career as a slo-pitch shortstop. I golf badly, ski infrequently and haven't replaced my racquetball racquet since 1988, when it blew off the back of the moving truck.

But suddenly I find myself immersed in jockdom, expected to make intelligent conversation (an impossibility, to be sure, when we're discussing sports) about Eric Lindros' $240 gazillion salary and whether the ball was hit fair or bounced foul, as if it really matters.

I even went to my first football game recently and had a perfectly lovely time sitting in the sunshine recalling ancient history lessons about the Christians and the lions while a bunch of triangular-shaped men scrambled around trying to snatch bits of artificially turfed real estate from each other.

I'm no psychologist, but my recent observations of this testosterone-driven industry have left me with a number of inescapable conclusions.

First, contrary to what TSN and ESPN would have us believe, there are really only three sports in the world, and infinite aberrations on the theme.

There's the I-can-go-faster-than-you-can sports (horse, car, motorcycle, ski, foot and camel racing), the I'm-bigger-than-you-and-I'm-going-to-pound-the-snot-out-of-you sports (wrestling, boxing, judo, karate and sumo wrestling), and lastly, of course, the I've-got-the-ball-and-you-can't-have-it sports (football, baseball, basketball, hockey and everything else except golf, which really isn't a sport and only for some of us can be considered a skill).

Of course, there is a fourth category, if we want to include the Honey-I'll-get-to-it-later sport practised by the other 97 per cent of the male population who don't get paid unruly amounts of cash to keep track of statistics like how many times Devon White has struck out in his last 4,946 times at bat but who do so anyway for reasons completely unknown to the rest of us.

The second conclusion I've drawn, which makes me at least as smart as Carl Lewis, is that it's all about money. Increasingly larger amounts of money.

Players want more money. They get it from the owners. (Unless they're independently employed like amateur skiers and race car drivers, who get it from their sponsors in exchange for plastering their bodies and vehicles with labels like well-travelled motorhomes. Or, if they're *real* creative, like golfer Payne Stewart, they can get owners of *other* sports to pay them to cross-dress.)

Owners want more money from the TV networks for the privilege of broadcasting the games. The TV networks want more money from the advertisers to cover the annual increases in broadcasting privileges.

And the advertisers want more money from us.

Which means the price of Cheerios is about to skyrocket. Thank you Eric Lindros.

SO MANY SPORTS CHANNELS,
SO LITTLE TIME

April 17, 1994

Each year at about this time a very odd phenomenon afflicts one half of one half of the human species in North America.

It arrives with little warning and its early symptoms are barely perceptible, but one day, without warning and when you least expect it, there it is.

A second television set appears as if by magic, sprouting from the top of your first, a second glass eye beaming monosyllabic interviews, statistics and images of Don Cherry's newest necktie into your living room, and with a sinking heart you realize it's snuck up on you once more.

It's playoff time.

Scrupulous polling of the male half of the species indicates not all men are so devoted to Canada's national pastime and Tampa's newest bloodsport that they would be so bold, but neither do they see anything wrong with dual viewing. No doubt they secretly envy those with such ambidextrous eyeballs.

The other half are not only highly skilled in the art of watching two hockey games simultaneously, they have indulged in the practise since their frat boy days. They were early proponents of the need for Canada's national broadcaster to air on two separate channels, and in 1974 were already well acquainted with the Saturday night joy of watching Habs games with the sound silenced atop the Flyers with full volume.

The advent of the remote control was heralded as a breakthrough in modern science, allowing them to alter volume and channels without disturbing the fine layer of dust that falls upon them in viewing mode. With one in each hand they can zap at will, like the gunslingers of yesteryear. A momentous goal or righteous fight on the small screen can be immediately transferred to the bigger screen, an annoying commercial on the big screen muted instantaneously.

The introduction of TSN and ESPN and Sportsdesk means they can enjoy highlights and replays of those 637 games they missed while focused on the two for which they've invested heavily in the local playoff pools.

In recent years, however, the expansion of hockey into Anaheim, Hawaii and Outer Mongolia means the year-end ritual of competing for the cup starts earlier and lasts longer, thus creating a conundrum for people whose previous choices were limited to which games to watch on which

TV. Now they are faced with option overload. Which games in which sports will get their deserved attention on Sunday afternoon?

Will it be hockey on the big screen and the Masters on the small? Is the small screen sufficient in size to actually see the little white ball on green grass, or it is better suited to the little black puck on white ice? What happens when the Blue Jays are engaged in a double header while the Leafs are duking it out with the Blackhawks? Women's hockey, World Cup Curling, NBA finals and what will happen when football season starts?

Will we witness an implosion of circuitry -- both cerebral and electronic -- or the purchase of yet another TV?

RIDING ON THE BUMPER CARS OF LIFE

February 9, 1993

Everyone, at one time or another, has either personally been involved in or knows someone else who's been involved in a relationship they liken to a roller coaster -- exhilarating highs, heart-stopping plunges, unexpected twists, turns and, inevitably, the Abrupt Stop. With lots of squealing brakes.

Without relationships like these, women's magazines would cease to publish and the bottom would drop out of the self-help book market. But if you think about it, every pairing has, in one way or another, a counterpart on a carnival midway.

There's the roller coaster -- up and down, around and around. Adrenalin junkies and people with otherwise really boring lives have a hard time getting off these ones. When they do, they usually can't wait to get back on. They *like* queasy stomachs and shaky knees, and there is absolutely nothing that can be done for these people except wait for them to grow up.

The only thing worse than the roller coaster relationship is the Drop of Doom -- one painful, brief, non-stop
plunge to rock bottom, complete with lots of screaming,
gnashing of teeth and white-lipped terror. And when it's
over, you wonder why you even bothered.

Some people, for reasons known only to themselves,
seem to like romances like The Rotor, where you just get
spun around, stuck to the wall and you want to throw up
when you get off. Go figure.

In the same vein, how about those bumper car
relationships, where you and the object of your affection
keep taking high-speed runs at each other, collide and
bounce apart at whiplash speed like negatively-charged at-
oms. (This, for many of us, is called dating.)

Then there's the Haunted House, where both partners ride around in the dark, being constantly surprised by
skeletons that pop out of nowhere.

And *those* are the exciting ones. Some people spend
most of their lives on the merry-go-round and consider the
never-ending pursuit of the brass (or gold) ring the main
point of the whole exercise.

Others prefer to go through life on the pony ride,
plodding along in endless circles, looking and feeling as put-
upon as the long-suffering beast of burden with whom they
are paired.

Ah, you wonder, what about the Tunnel of Love?
What about it? When was the last time you saw one on a
carnival midway? My own suspicion is that it was something
invented for the *Archie* comic books so we'd have the
illusion of romance without actually ever having to see
Betty or Veronica in the back seat of a Chevy.

Personally I think the best ride has to be the ferris
wheel. Occasional starts and stops, but overall panoramic
vistas and, unless you're riding with some jerk who likes to
rock the chair, the adrenalin is kept to a minimum. Long,
slow ups and downs that you can see coming a mile away but
still make your pulse race because, hey, isn't that what it's
all about?

A DOG'S BEST FRIEND IS HER MAN

March 30, 1993

In recent months I've come to know what it must feel like to be a stepmother.

It seems that when I entered my current relationship I inadvertently took on co-parenting duties for one slightly aging, highly intelligent and occasionally devious canine who had -- until then -- been an extremely obedient companion for her lifelong owner.

Actually, she still is obedient for him. It's the stepmother she's testing, a committed feline aficionado who used to fix Brutus the cat his own soft boiled egg for Sunday brunch and allowed him to dine on the kitchen table. (Brutus expired two years ago of kidney failure, not clogged arteries, and I only did it because he would have eaten mine anyway.)

Obviously I've never much been comfortable with the role of disciplinarian, but I find myself reconsidering its merits.

The first turf war was over the front seat of the van. For years Saxson the Wonderdog had sole proprietorship and a great view, but when I abruptly entered her serene existence she was banished to the rear. No amount of hurt looks and sloppy, pleading kisses for the driver would prevail upon him to relent. I, however, suffered an extreme case of the post-Catholic guilts and promptly invited her to share the upholstery.

Big mistake. On our last road trip I spend four hours pinned down by a 30-pound mutt who made like a large cat, stretched out on my lap with her head on my shoulder, her hind quarters on my knees and her little doggie elbows digging into my thighs with every righthand turn.

Then there was the bed, an ultra-king-sized monstrosity that seemed far too large for just two people while poor Sax curled up on a blanket on the floor. I invited her up.

She was hesitant at first, but quickly warmed to the idea. Did I say warmed? She embraced it wholeheartedly, as if it were her royal birthright. Now I have a nightly wrestling match with a two-foot beast who somehow fills an entire acre of mattress from corner to corner and only cedes ground with great reluctance. Each morning I wake up with an active dog tongue in my left ear, a sign, I am told, of her great affection for me. Wonderful.

More recently, however, I am seeing signs of overt defiance. She has misinterpreted my attempts at conciliation for outright softness, and regardless of whatever doggie affection she has for me her little canine brain processes the word MARSHMALLOW whenever she hears my voice.

I tried to take her for a W-A-L-K, a word that ordinarily excites her so much we have to spell it if it's not something that's going to happen immediately.

We got as far as the front lawn when Sax realized that He Who She *Will* Obey wasn't there with us. She planted her butt on the ground and refused to budget.

"C'mon Saxson," I pleaded. "Let's go for a WALK!"

Thump, thump, went the tail.

"Saxson, COME!" I commanded in my very best, imitation authoritative voice.

Thump, thump. Bark, bark.

"SAXSON!!!"

Then she turned daintily and pranced away, tail held high in the air like the animal approximation of an upraised finger.

I swear she was grinning.

SHOPPING CAN BE HAZARDOUS
TO YOUR LOVE LIFE

December 15, 1992

Ah, Christmas. Feel that mounting panic in the air. Only 10 shopping days left and I haven't even started the annual ravaging of the chequing account. I think I'm in denial.

This year my own personal panic is heightened by a new dilemma of the male persuasion. It's of small consolation to know I share this equal opportunity angst with partnered people the world over -- those of us who haven't a hot clue what to buy their mate, spouse, boyfriend, girlfriend, POSSLQ or Significant Other.

I'm out of practice. Last year at this time we were both complacently single. We didn't even know the other existed. This year we are (drum roll) Shopping For Each Other, a symbolic ritual fraught with undertones, overtones and endless possibilities for Screwing Up.

I know of what I speak. I once had a boyfriend who bought me a steam iron for our first Christmas together. I was offended at his lack of romance. (For the record, I bought him an expensive watch which he promptly lost on Boxing Day.) The next year he bought me a wisp of black lace from Tarts 'R' Us. I was *really* offended. The relationship was doomed.

Right now we -- the new He and I -- are trying very hard to avoid these kinds of communicative failures. We are scrutinizing every facet of each other's lives, eating habits, wardrobe sizes and listening tastes. We are seeking hints and harassing mutual friends. We are asking outright.

It's of little help. We're at that awkward stage where romance is still fresh but we need a new blender, where familiarity has lessened the need to declare one's passion with tangible evidence, but a waffle iron under the tree would shatter some illusions.

'Tis a fragile balance indeed between long-stemmed roses and power drills.

I've already discarded a dozen ideas, simply because each bears its own mixed message. If I buy him aftershave, am I implying I don't like the brand he wears? A CD I think he would like suggests I don't like the music *he* does.

Will a pass to the fitness centre imply I pine for *svelte?*

Car accessories? Too impersonal. Jewelry? Doesn't wear it (thank god). Clothes? See above re: possible implication of present dissatisfaction with his attire. A year's supply of golf balls? What if I overestimate?

What he really needs is a girlfriend with a better imagination.

He, on the other hand, faces an even more perilous decision. We women are always saying we're *so* much easier to buy for, but you men know we women attach *so* much more significance to (drum roll) The Gift. And the First Official Gift is about as significant as it gets.

Will it be something we treasure always? Will it be something we can brag about to friends, proof positive that Huge Romance is alive and thriving? Will it forever conjure up fond memories of Our First Christmas? Sigh. Or will it be something joked about in years to come, old what's-his-name and the year you found your very own Super Soaker under the tree.

Beware, oh fellow shoppers. 'Tis the season to be careful.

A WOMAN'S GUIDE TO SURVIVING THE SERIES

October 19, 1993

It's that time of year again, fellow females, that time when our mates, partners, husbands and boyfriends take up permanent residence in front of the tube to revel in that annual bonding ritual known as the World Series.

By some interplanetary quirk, this event dovetails perfectly with the beginning of the hockey season and the middle of the football season, thereby guaranteeing that at any given hour of any given day a game of some monumental significance in one of those three sports will be on and your loved one will be unable to perform any function more challenging than berating myopic umpires or phoning even the remotest of acquaintances in Philadelphia to chortle about Them Jays.

This is not a phenomena limited to the male of the species. A lifetime ago I knew dozens of women who dragged themselves out of bed to watch Chuck wed Di at 4 a.m. CST, and heaven help whoever gets between me and the season premiere of *Picket Fences* this Friday. (A travel day for Them Jays, thank God.)

No, we are all slaves to our own particular passions. Few among us have never been blinded by the flickering light.

If you are relatively new in your relationship and find yourself unavoidably trapped with someone suffering from Pennant Stupor, you might be content to sit alongside and become well-versed in such things as sweet spots, bullpens, ERAs and the reasons for the third base coach's continual groping of his upper torso.

Altogether, this is not a bad plan of action. You can learn more in one night about the relative merits of grass vs. Astroturf, sliders vs. fastballs and the maximum number of wads of Double Bubble that can be chewed at one time than you ever previously imagined.

You can also be taking vicarious pleasure in the knowledge that all those Kim Campbell election spots interspersed with the Ford truck ads and the bullpen close-ups are swinging his moods around like a yo-yo and now he, too, has some inkling of what PMS is all about.

If, on the other hand, you are a somewhat more established partner and your mate has begun regarding you as part of the general living room decor, you may be tempted to express your neglected frustration by drawing audible comparisons between his physique and that of the Philly players. Not a wise move, lest you forever want to be bracing yourself for retaliation when *Roseanne* comes on. What goes around generally comes around.

Far better you should channel your energies into something constructive. If you have such a hankering, you could dye your hair a bright orange, revamp your wardrobe, trade in the car and wallpaper the bedroom and have at least a week to get used to it all before he notices.

You could also do the bulk of your Christmas shopping before next Sunday and chances are good your absence from the living room will not be missed.

For those of you with the means, this is the perfect time to think about the perfect Christmas present for that special someone -- a couple of tickets to next season's Series, so at this time next year, you'll have the house all to yourself.

UNSOLICITED ADVICE FOR
THE SOON-TO-BE-WED

June 22, 1993

I've been thinking a lot about marriage lately. (Boy, what wouldn't I give to be able to see my mother's face as she reads this?)

I've been thinking about it a lot because it seems every second day well-meaning but seriously misinformed people congratulate me on my pending nuptials. These people several weeks ago read my young colleague David Wilson's column about *his* approaching date with permanent commitment and jumped to an erroneous conclusion.

It is *he* who is trying to match cummerbund to bow tie and elicit from his parents a guest list containing at least 10 recognizable names. It is *he* who is suddenly confronted with monumental decisions about embossed matchbook covers and color coordinated floral arrangements. (It is also he who is a little upset that our readers don't recognize his byline after a year with this paper, but I think it's just a little pre-wedding crankiness.)

I personally am still enjoying an unblemished marital record, thank you very much. But seeing as how I am somewhat of an expert on the subject (in part because I have been dating the same person for an entire year, in and of itself something of a minor miracle, and also because I was raised by married people) I am going to offer a little advice to young David.

(As we speak, committed veterans are rolling their eyes and saying, 'Yeah, right. What does *she* know?' Let me pose this rhetorical question: Is not a catch and release angler as knowledgeable as the one who catches and keeps? Hmmm?)

The first thing a pre-wedded person should know is that Inappropriate Disposal of Dirty Socks is grounds for divorce in eight provinces, and if your betrothed comes with her own laundry hamper, or if you get one as a wedding present, its use therefore becomes mandatory.

After marriage you will likely be sharing the same quarters. There are several ways you can learn to maintain a harmonious household, the most obvious of which is to look for clues. If she leaves the toilet seat down, this is probably the way she likes it. A vacuum cleaner left in the centre of the rug does not necessarily mean she was suddenly interrupted and didn't finish. If she doesn't allow the dog to eat the leftovers from the good china, nor should you.

See how easy this is?

Money is apparently another popular source of contention for married people, and while I am certainly no fiscal wizard I do know that it's generally not a good idea to buy a new set of golf clubs when the nice folks at Visa have called 32 times in the last week. Or if you've just forgotten your anniversary.

The most important thing you should know about, however, if the need for communication. Not just for the extraction of practical information such as how to use that vacuum cleaner, but for the sharing of feelings, the importance of which, having gotten to the engagement stage, you should be fully aware.

If she says something like, "Darling, we have to talk," it is generally not a good idea to merely nod a lot and make um-*hmm* noises, because she could slip in a trick question like, "Darling, are you having an affair?" and then all of those souvenir, embossed color coordinated matchbook covers would have been totally wasted.

WHO SAYS CARS AND BOATS ARE FEMALE?

July 6, 1993

Last week a full-page ad in a certain broadsheet daily newspaper in a metropolitan community downstream from Canmore exhorted readers to come to a Canada Day party to "Help Celebrate Her Birthday?"

Who's her? Since when did our country become a woman? Last time I checked, a full 49 per cent of our population was still of the male gender, one of whom was undoubtedly the writer of this bit of ad copy because the tendency to assign a female pronoun to inanimate objects is purely a guy thing. Trust me on this. I have spent a lifetime noticing this little macho idiosyncrasy simply because it has the same effect on me as a bit of tin foil stuck in my molars.

Every fish pulled out of every lake and stream in this country has been female, according to the anglers who are immediately compelled to exclaim: "She's a beaut!"

A long, soaring golf drive inevitably takes on female properties, when from the mouth of the golfer comes something along of the lines of, "Look at her go!"

(A variation on this would be the old standby, "Look at that baby go!" which, while strictly speaking is gender neutral, takes on definite female connotations because not a whole lot of guys would refer to something they consider masculine as "baby".)

"She's running well," or "She's idling a bit rough," they will say about their car, even if it is a long, phallic-shaped Corvette.

"She's loaded," does not necessarily mean a wealthy woman is in the vicinity, merely that the car, truck, motorcycle or stereo system to which they refer comes with a lot of options.

Even the lawnmower becomes female when "she's out of gas".

Boats are inevitably female and have been since long before Maritime songwriters declared, "I'se the b'ye that build the boat and I'se the b'ye that sails her."

A certain someone near and dear to me even decided last year his hairy leg was somehow female when, after minor surgery, he daily updated me on its progress with "She's a little sore today," or "She's feeling better".

Mother Nature aside, when did wind, rain, snow, sleet, hail and tornadoes take on feminine characteristics? Why is "she" hot, cold, wet or snowy? If the U.S. Weather Service can finally get with the program and assign male names to half of all hurricanes, how come the other 99.99 per cent of the planet can't stop saying "She's blowing up a storm?"

I don't have the foggiest. My best guess is that it's some kind of manifestation of hormonal confusion. Extensive research would no doubt show that most men are not even aware that they do this, and once made aware would say they don't have a hot clue why.

(My second best guess is that men do this when confronted with anything they don't fully understand, like the vagaries of nature, the workings of internal combustion engines or women as a species.)

What I *would* like to know, however, is this: If everything in the world is in some way, shape or form female, how come we're not running the place?

THE MYSTERIES OF LIFE AND MIXMASTERS

May 24, 1994

Do you own an electric hand mixer? Go, right now, and check how many beaters you've got in the drawer. My guess is, if you've owned the mixer for more than six months, you will already have lost one beater. Not both, one. Singular.

Don't ask me why this is so. It could be that you've somehow displeased the kitchen gods. You may have been the victim of a kleptomaniac with a stainless steel fetish. My personal suspicion is that it's a manufacturers' conspiracy. At a certain point in the life of the mixer, one beater is programmed to dissolve in the dishwasher or disappear for eternity into its mechanical bowels. It's a clear case of built-in obsolescence, akin to vanishing socks in the clothes dryer and earrings in the jewelry box.

(And do they sell mixer blades separately? Of course not. Once one blade is gone, one must shell out another $29.95 for a new mixer, and if right now you don't have just one blade in the drawer you have three of them because you're clinging to the one from the last mixer in the futile hope it's going to fit the new machine.)

It's like a rite of passage, a measurement of longevity. You know you've been married a long time when...

Oddly enough, the missing mixer blade is a source of great amusement of younger women, the ones who've either just married or moved out on their own, the overly confident ones with gleaming new appliances, unchipped coffee mugs and two intact mixer blades. They approach the whole issue of disappearing turkey skewers and vanishing mixer blades with an air of arrogance, as if you have to *really* be some kind of moron to misplace something so integral to food preparation.

They are, as yet, oblivious to the proclivity of these blades to march off unassisted. (Or assisted, as the case may be. A good friend of mine, about to celebrate 25 years of wedded endurance, lost her latest blade when her husband borrowed the machine to mix paint. My mother had this problem too, and after 40 years and 37 mixer blades transplanted to the tool box has finally given up on the concept of whipped cream with the shortcake.)

One can almost measure one's journey to maturity by the mixer blade syndrome. We all start off cocky and confident, disdainful of those who are so unorganized they lose something as tangible as a mixer blade, until the day we awaken to discover ours has gone. And then, before you know it, you have a daughter-in-law or niece standing in your kitchen, rifling through the drawers and inquiring with that faint hint of superiority how you could *possibly* lose such a thing, and we want to kill her. But we don't, because we know something she doesn't. Her turn will come.

WOMEN SHOP. GUYS JUST BUY STUFF.

November 9, 1993

I confess I'm about to embark upon a journey that could have tremendously unpatriotic implications. I'm going shopping. In the U.S.A. Not on purpose -- I just happen to be going to the U.S.A. and I just happen to be taking some money and it just happens to be the month before Christmas and there just happens to be at least one shopping mall in this place where I am going and I may happen to visit it.

(I'm too embarrassed to tell you the exact location of this place because in truth it is somewhat tacky and has a lot of slot machines and golf courses and very few culturally redeeming features, except for a shrine to Liberace and a car that Al Capone once owned. But it's a cheap vacation and I am in desperate need of some R&R -- Retreat and Regrouping -- plus it has a GST-free mall.)

Comedienne Elaine Boosler several years ago did an outrageously funny skit on the shopping disparities between men and women. Women, she said, approach shopping as our prehistoric foremothers approached their hunting and gathering duties. We stalk, we search, we pounce and we bring home our treasures and display them as trophies.

Guys just buy stuff.

It's true. A guy will walk into a store and buy a pair of socks in 30 seconds flat, stick the bag in his pocket and promptly forget about it. Women, however, will spend hours tracking the perfect pair of pantyhose and, when located, have a desperate need to show them to someone. You get home, rifle them out of the package and hold them up proudly -- Look dear, won't these just *perfectly* match that plum taffeta skirt I bagged last week?

There are few women alive who can buy something and put it away without showing another soul what they have bought, even if it is a wholly disinterested male. It's genetically impossible.

Guys, on the other hand, feel no such need to brag about purchases. The women in their lives discover new additions to their partner's wardrobe as they're doing laundry or, if he happens to do his primary purchasing at Costco, as they're unpacking the groceries.

You'll seldom hear guys sitting around in a group reliving great shopping experiences (unless they involve boat motors or golf clubs) but we women can remember to the penny what we paid for any particular item in our closets, as well as precisely where it was purchased and what the sales clerk said when the purchase was taking place.

Women will spend months shopping without spending a cent. They stalk precise items like jewelry or scarves or blouses to match other items previously scored and mounted in the closet, and without having even glanced at those trophies in months can tell in a millisecond whether the new accessory will match. We carry mental fabric swatches around in our brains.

For most men, aimless shopping is an ordeal. For me, it's one of those luxuries one never has enough time to do in real life. So, starting Thursday, hunting season opens for me.

My mate and I may be going to the same location, but it would appear we'll be taking separate vacations.

Compatibility and the
Art of House Hunting

March 15, 1994

There are few things in this life more likely to test the strength of a relationship than house hunting. The desire or impetus to transplant yourself, your loved one and all of your worldly possessions from one set of walls to another is a true measure of compatibility.

Each person brings to a relationship a set of expectations and priorities, some of which are unknown even to themselves until confronted with another person's expectations and priorities.

This is when they learn the art of compromise, otherwise known as How to Fight Fair.

My Significant Other and I began our search for a new place to live about four months ago. One hundred and eighteen days later, having alternately rejected each others' choices, been rejected by prospective landlords or endorsed each others' choices but have taken so long to reach agreement that we've lost the place because someone else moved faster, we are still speaking, er, seeking the perfect abode.

He needs a garage. I need office space. He has too many tools. I have too many books. We have a dog and we smoke, which eliminates us from 98 per cent of the available rental accommodation in this town. (Talk about having two strikes against you.)

We have looked at houses. We have looked at condos. We have looked at apartments and we have looked at basement suites. They are either too old, too big, too small or too dark. Too many white walls remind me of suburbia, but funky old houses bring with them huge heating bills, he says. We are seriously considering pricing tents.

Not enough cupboard space. The carpet didn't match our couch. Insufficient parking space. Too far from downtown. No fireplace. Substandard views. You'd think we had

the availability of Calgary's housing stock from which to
choose, so picky are we being.

He likes big, wide open spaces inside a condo. I see
big space and immediately think -- vacuum cleaner. I love
big yards, and where I see room for vegetable and flower
gardens he thinks -- lawn mower.

Lest you think we are hopelessly trapped in tradi-
tional roles, he wants to trade the "privilege" of hanging all
the wall art in exchange for his having sole domain in the
arrangement of the kitchen.

There are few things in this world I am less talented
at than interior design, and infinitely more things I would
rather do than be entirely responsible for the decoration of
our new walls -- if we ever get any.

The really scary part is that once we *do* find a new
place to live, we are both going to bring things out of
storage. What if he's got one of those wagon wheel coffee
tables like Bruno Kirby in *When Harry Met Sally*? What if
he laughs at my collection of Japanese masks and won't let
me hang my *Raiders of the Lost Ark* poster in the bathroom?
What if we're compatible but our possessions are not?

What if we have to wallpaper something?

WHY WOMEN KEEP THE
HOME FIRES BURNING

October 4, 1994

The Cold War is on again, in every home in every town in
every country in the northern hemisphere.

The weather turns wintry and the thermostat starts
bouncing up and down like a yo-yo. She likes it tolerable, he
craves sub-Arctic. She layers on the socks and sweaters, he
cranks open the window, inhaling deeply and coating his
lungs with ice crystals. She throws another log on the first

and tries to get used to turning the pages of her book with mittens on her hands.

During the winter a lot more baking gets done. He thinks it's because she loves him. She sees it as a legitimate excuse to keep the oven on all day.

She no longer wonders why the first gift her mother-in-law ever gave her was a pair of heavy woolen slippers, nor why knitting afghans seemed like such a popular pastime among so many of her married friends.

There is a fallacy that exists in the minds of most men. They have long since bought into the notion that women have an extra layer of fat and therefore it's okay to keep the temperature in the house around seven degrees.

Wrong.

If we have an extra layer of fat, it's in our heads. That's why we agreed to spend the rest of our lives sharing living space with these guys, even after we are well acquainted with their fondness for frigid air.

For six months a year the struggle rages. She deliberately walks around without socks for 10 seconds before leaping into bed and placing her icy feet square in the middle of his back, just to hear him yelp. See, she gloats, it's too cold in here!

He quits grumbling about her sleeping in socks and sweatshirts and pins the heating bill to the front of the fridge door with the five-digit "amount owning" circled in red. She buys another duvet and another cord of firewood.

She accuses him of subterfuge when she finds all the heat registers in their sleeping quarters turned off. He is reproachful each morning to find she's awakened in the wee hours to shut the window and scrape the frost from the pillows.

They agree to compromise and set the thermometer midway between what she finds comfortable and what he feels is acceptable. In the fine art of compromise, they are both miserable.

It's surprising that dating agencies don't twig onto this and start matching people up according to their basal body temperatures. The divorce rate would plummet as fast as the mercury. Compatible comfort zones should be a

mandatory point of agreement during pre-marital counsel-
ling.

Never mind whether you agree on managing your
finances and what religion you plan to raise any future
offspring in -- can you live with 15 degrees Celsius?

Actually, there's probably a great business opportunity here. If someone can come up with a way to make
pajamas made of fleece and flannelette look sexy, there's
probably a million men who would buy them.

FOR BETTER OR WORSE UNTIL
WE'RE OUT OF CLEAN CLOTHES

June 21, 1994

It starts with a single sock in the middle of the floor. Or
dirty underwear reposing under the bed. Or mildewed clothes
that sit in the washer for several days, forgotten and unnoticed.

Sometimes it's a white blouse thrown in with the
brand new, indigo-dyed blue jeans, or a fine wool sweater
tossed into the dryer to tumble around until it fits a Barbie
doll.

It's not sex or money or even religious differences
that destroy relationships. It's laundry wars.

A filled-to-overflowing hamper which both parties
studiously ignore becomes symbolic of something bigger, an
indication that both parties feel they're doing more around
the house than the other. "It's *his* turn," she hisses mentally, while he stocks up on new socks, determined to
outwait his mate.

The laundry basket develops a momentum of its own,
moving slowly from the corner of the bedroom to the top of
the stairs, then, step by step and day by day, down to the
washer. It rests there for several days until someone tosses
the dirty clothes into the machine with a handful of soap

and walks away, secure in the knowledge that their partner will somehow know by osmosis that there are clothes that must be transferred to the dryer.

A week later, finally noticing that the empty basket beside the washer has not moved, the partner peeks under the lid and tries to gauge, without the use of carbon-dating, the approximate length of time the clothes have been there. And then starts the washer again, just to get rid of the musty odor. It is thus that clothes get washed six times between wearings.

Drying the clothes has a similar protocol, wherein they are subjected to multiple cycles because they're so wrinkled from sitting around for endless days they must be repeatedly tumbled to fluff them up, shake them out or else, god forbid, they'll all have to be ironed.

Once the clothes have actually left the dryer and made their way back to the bedroom, there is usually another delay of several days' duration while both partners root through the mound, finding whatever socks, T-shirts or underwear are necessary for that day only.

Neither will take responsibility for finding semi-permanent homes in drawers or shelves for the rest of the garments.

(Sometimes, on the rare occasions when one does fold and stow, a subtle form of one-upmanship occurs, and the second partner, not to be outdone, refolds the clothes into a more appropriate configuration. Why this partner did not just fold the clothes themselves in the first place remains a mystery.)

After several days of harvesting fresh undergarments, the few clothes remaining in the basket become the bottom layer for the new dirty clothes, the assumption being that if you've seen the same shirt in the basket for six days it must be dirty. The cycle begins anew.

One begins to think longingly of public laundromats, where limitations on spare change and time force one to start and finish the laundry all in the same day, regardless of whose turn it is.

A Spinster's Guide to
Wedding Survival

June 19, 1994

I am going to write a book. I am going to call it *A Spinster's Guide to Wedding Survival*. It is going to have a lot of chapters, but the best one is going to be called *K.I.S.S.* -- *Keep It Simple, Stupid*.

Chapter One -- Choose Well. If you are a chronic procrastinator, it is never a good idea to choose another one for your lifetime mate, because chances are you will never get around to actually doing anything beyond asking and answering the big "Will you ?" question.

Chapter Two -- Announcing Your Betrothal. Within a few days of the news leaking out, you will be faced with a barrage of questions, or rather, you will be faced with the same three questions over and over. They are as follows: Are you keeping your own name? What's your dress like? And, amazingly enough (although I suppose if one waits until one is 37 to finally wed it shouldn't come as all that much of a shock) Are you pregnant?

The first and last questions are fairly easy to deal with in a relatively tactful manner. It's the second one that's the killer. Until you find something to wear, your mother will not sleep.

Chapter Three -- Deciding How to Wed. Do you do it quietly, with one or two close friends, or in front of all those friends and relatives who have reacted to the news of your betrothal with outbursts like, "Good grief! Hell must finally be frozen over!"

Chapter Four -- Planning the Event. Having decided one cannot disappoint all those kith and kin, the next step is to find a facility capable of holding all of the above. It's generally a good idea to go with the one that has an extremely efficient food and beverage manager who's been through this before and turn your life over to him or her. Do whatever he or she says.

Chapter Five -- Finding the Appropriate Attire. If you are a true spinster, you will not have spent a lot of time envisioning yourself as a bride, whereas your mother will have spent a lifetime doing just that. Let her take sole control of your attire for the day. Trust me on this. She knows just what you want. One of our wedding party now has something to wear. Except shoes.

Chapter Six -- K.I.S.S. Apparently there are a zillion details that go into this shtick that will trip you up at the last moment, or so say the bridal bibles. Do not even be tempted at the magazine racks. These are merely large, glossy packets of advertisements disguised as magazines. They will try to convince you your wedding will be a total failure unless you have a $79.95 bone-handled silver knife with which to cut the cake. (Uh oh. We forgot the cake.)

The one bit of practical advice you can glean from these magazines is the importance of making a list. We made our list a long time ago: Flowers. Rings. License. Music man. Suit for groom. So far, only the music man's been checked off. (See Chapter Three re: efficient food and beverage manager.)

In about six weeks' time, roughly 100 people are going to show up at a local establishment in their Sunday finest to see me and my taller half do something neither of us has done before.

We will not disappoint them, but chances are we'll be late and they're all going to be better dressed than we.

PLANNING D-DAY WAS PROBABLY EASIER

July 26, 1994

Wedding Day Minus Five. The stress level around our house is climbing faster than the mercury. A little Pre-Marital Syndrome, if you will.

Murphy has moved in. Whatever could go wrong has gone wrong, or is threatening to in mere moments. Each day we awaken and realize the countdown to chaos is that much closer.

We're at that point where we're seriously wondering why we just didn't head to Hawaii, wed on a beach and surprise all the folks and friends upon our return. We were told -- no, we were encouraged -- by all those married folks who've been there and done that to skip the dinner, dancing and floral arrangements and just skip town. As Lily Tomlin once said, "Maybe if we started listening to it, history would stop repeating itself."

No, we're embarking down a well-trod path, strewn with the horror stories of friends and families who've all got their tales to tell. Drunken uncles and beastly photographers. Misplaced bouquets and DJs with a passion for disco. Outbreaks of chicken pox, laryngitis and agoraphobia.

There's a common theme to these recollections, that being that none of them can recollect with any kind of clarity the actual wedding itself. They do, however, remember vividly the frantic weeks leading up to it and the sense of relief they felt when it was all over.

"Do you take this frazzled, stressed-out basket case to be your lawful wedded wife?"

Weddings, it would seem, are the ultimate marital test. If you can get through the planning and successful execution of such an event with a shared sense of humor and your relationship intact, you're well on your way.

The out of town guests have already started arriving, bunked down in hotels, motels, campgrounds and bed and breakfasts throughout the Bow Valley. Keeping track of them is nearly as easy as remembering where we put the marriage license.

The dog, an integral part of the wedding party, has finally figured out I am about to become a permanent fixture in her life and is rebelling as obnoxiously as an adolescent daughter. I suspect she's thus far been hoping I was merely a passing fancy and I'd disappear as abruptly as I entered her complacent life.

Friends of my hubby-to-be are still taking him aside for the reassuring little pep talk that go something like this: "You know, there's still time to get out of this."

Mine are keeping track of the dwindling days more fervently than I. "Hey," they greet me on the phone, "only five more days to go!" Gee, thanks, I'd completely forgotten.

Now I know why people are only supposed to get married once. And I'm beginning to fully appreciate the need for a honeymoon. A week from today, I will be motoring westward for two weeks of camping, hiking, biking and golf. In my suitcase will be my brand new copy of *Is There Life After Marriage?*

In my absence, my capable colleague David Wilson will be the captain of this little paper. It'll be good for him. It's been a year since his wedding, and he's probably forgotten what real stress feels like.

EARLY TO BED AND EARLY TO RISE MAKES ONE CRANKY

December 6, 1994

Every night I go to bed with the man of my dreams.

Every morning I wake up with a total jerk.

Nor am I alone. Not, I hasten to add, that there are other people in bed with my spouse and me, but I do believe there are dozens, nay, hundreds of other women in my position. Probably even men, I dare say.

He whistles. He hums. He smiles *way* too much. Another month and I am certain he will chirp. He is so disgustingly *cheerful* in the morning I am seriously considering lobbying for a town bylaw to have him -- and those of his ilk -- banished to Banff until the noonday sun reaches its zenith. The workaday world should not begun until all of us are ready for it. Not some of us, all of us.

Probably more important than the how-warm-should-this-house-be-in-the-dead-of-winter test, the inner body clock should be the real litmus of marital compatibility. In sickness and in health, for richer and for poorer and only if both of you are ready to face the world at a decent and agreed-upon hour, like 10 a.m.

My body clock is set to the post-midnight mode, his to the 5 a.m. *Sportsdesk*. Mine has been like this for most of my adult life and so, I suspect, has his. Yes, I knew what he was like before I married him. I was seriously hoping some of my pre-noon grumpiness would rub off, but thus far my snarling efforts have been in vain.

I function extremely well in those wee, tiny hours when even the lowliest paid of the CBC announcers has signed off for the night. At 2 a.m. or 3 a.m. I am a positive genius. Those of you who have tried to contact me in the office before 10 a.m. -- and those of you who have succeeded -- can attest to the fact that my ability to form a coherent thought doesn't usually begin until other people have achieved a half day's work, my spouse included.

He, on the other hand, *loves* mornings. He greets the day with a smile on his face and a song on his lips. (Figuratively speaking, of course. If he actually started whistling *Zippidee-doo-dah* at 6 a.m. I'm sure I'd be filing for an annulment under that six-month warranty period.)

He critiques the sunrises for me, just to apprise me of that which I am missing. He harbors hope that eventually I will realize the truthfulness of his admonishments that I am "missing the best part of the day".

I suspect, judging by literary and legendary reference, this discrepancy between early risers and the rest of the so-called civilized world has been around for a long time. But "early to bed and early to rise", last time I checked, specifically applied to men only in the health and wisdom department. And as for that early bird getting the worm bit, even the nuthatches who frequent my backyard feeder have learned not to expect anything fresh before 10 a.m.

To be fair, those of us who are late night workers and late morning risers must drive the rest of you early

morning people nuts. Well, all I can say about that is --
good.

Then we're even.

THE CASE OF THE DISAPPEARING WALLS

Forever is truly a strange concept. One minute you're
thinking about the m-m-m-marriage word and trying to
mentally wrap the idea of eternity around conjugal love and
fidelity, and the next thing you know you're sitting in the
bank manager's office and now there's *three* of you talking
about m-m-m-m-ortgages.

And your mind goes back to that word again --
forever.

Worse yet, the bank manager's *nodding*, as if she's
been placed under a spell and sitting before her are *not* the
two most financially irresponsible individuals placed on this
earth but a couple of fine, upstanding citizens eager to begin
paying municipal taxes and fixing their own furnace.

What has happened to us? What have we done?
(Other than write a few cheques with more zeroes on them
than either of us has ever seen on the same piece of paper,
we seem to have taken one giant plunge into middle-aged
responsibility in one heck of a hurry. Shudder.)

We have bought a foundation and a floor plan. And a
hunk of property to put it on. And now we have to create
the home of our* dreams in a very few short months.

(*Editor's note: "Our" in this case is quickly starting
to encompass every electrician, plumber, finishing carpenter
or "been there, done that" person in this valley whose input
my mate has sought and received. Thank you all very much.
If he comes home one more time and announces that "we"
-- and I haven't been part of the conversation -- have
decided to build one more deck or vault one more ceiling, I
hold you all responsible.)

I'm an off-the-rack kind of shopper, be it blue jeans or house plans. He, I belatedly learn, hankers for tailor-made. My evenings are now spent complacently hogging the remote control, while he huddles over the kitchen table, a man possessed with Home Improvements.

He has now measured every stick of furniture and major appliance we own and translated feet into itty bitty bits of an inch, transferred his calculations onto a scale drawing of "our" new tiny mansion and used liquid paper to completely erase, move or otherwise alter what walls I thought I was buying.

The walk-in closet off the master bedroom is quickly becoming two hooks on the wall ("dead space," says he) and the bathroom may yet have to be relocated to the backyard. I am about to draw an itty bitty barbed wire fence around the pantry on his itty bitty scale drawing, lest he determine it, also, to be just another empty air pocket just waiting to be whited-out.

What fun. And we haven't even gotten to the carpet, paint, linoleum, tile, trim colors, kitchen cabinets or counter tops. At this rate, World War III should break out just about the time we get around to choosing faucets.

His horoscope for the next three months will read: "Domestic harmony will take a back burner while more pressing renovation plans take precedence."

Mine will be: "Bite your tongue. Again."

The hardest question of all will be whether we will be still be sharing sleeping quarters by the time we're finished.

We hope so. After all, we've taken a vow -- 'Til debt do us part.

SECTION THREE
THE FASHION GODS ARE NOT AMUSED

Fashion Fluctuations on
The Road to Canmore

September 23, 1991

Remember when Arnie Becker's therapist told him he was suffering from Fear of Furniture? The other night my friends told me I have Fear of Wardrobe.

Okay, so I *have* changed my style a few times over the years. Okay, so I *do* have a bunch of new clothes right now, as we speak, all purchased specifically to live in Canmore. It is NOT Fear of Commitment. It's a finely-honed adapting mechanism developed after years of taking on new challenges in new locations. New clothes to blend into new surroundings. Survival of the fittest, sartorially speaking.

I started out as an uptown kinda girl. High-heeled leather boots, thin suede gloves that cost most of my food budget but looked great with that little cashmere scarf that barely kept my earlobes pliable.

I suffered proudly for the sake of fashion in Winnipeg (an oxymoron, I know, but let's let it pass), dressed for success and coolly calculating my next leg up on the corporate ladder of success.

A few years and several professional setbacks later, I ended up at the *Edmonton Sun*, doing a two-year stint on the three-to-midnight copy editing desk, surrounded by men who took literally their job description of "rim pig". I camouflaged myself appropriately in sweatshirts and jeans and packed away the high heels and silk blouses, fairly certain that someday I would again work in a civilized environment where the man at the next desk wasn't called Jimmy the Geek and no one would know me as The Dwarf. (Vertically challenged, thank you very much.)

When I finally fled, I ended up in Japan, teaching "Bobby's new friend Tommy knows how to play soccer" to adolescent lads previously limited to "I'm-fine-sank-you-beddy-muchie!" It was exhilarating. Everybody bowed and smiled every time I entered a room. Everybody thought I was of normal height. Everybody admired my wardrobe, which was just like everybody else's neutral-colored A-line skirts with sensible, low-heeled shoes.

And now here I am in Paradise, comparison shopping for long underwear and faced daily with a wardrobe decision that see-saws between which pair of Levis to wear with which woolly sweater.

I just spent $65 on a pair of knee-high white boots with solid rubber tire-tread soles, seriously thermal liners and hot pink laces (for the feminine touch) that in my distant youth were known as s--t-kicking stompers that no self-respecting career woman would be caught dead in -- frostbite be damned.

I'm pretty proud of them. They give me a sense of security when I walk down the unlighted gravel road to my friends' house, confident that the brilliant white and neon pink will scare off any bears I might encounter.

(Lurking rapists have been replaced by grizzly bears as the thing I am most afraid of meeting now on dark, deserted streets.)

My, how things change. The other day I unpacked the boxes I stuffed three years ago in Edmonton and unearthed the attire I thought I'd need again some day. Anybody in the market for 10 pairs of size seven, slightly-used four-inch spiked pumps in a variety of colors?

Stability -- what a concept!

No way. Uh-uh.
Not me. Not Spandex.

April 27, 1993

It's nearly that time of year again, that season when those who can do, those who shouldn't try anyway and those who won't cringe at the sight of either.

Just a couple more warm, sunny, Spring-like days
and the dreaded Spandex people will be out in force again, in
both of their equally offensive variations.

Some will parade their sleek, sinewy cyclists' legs
along our fair boulevards, oblivious to the envious, seething
stares from less shapely passersby. Others will avert their
eyes at every store window lest they actually catch a reflec-
tion of themselves stuffed into elastic shorts that fit like
sausage casings.

All will frustrate, annoy and cruelly taunt those of us
whose commitment to the stationary bike this past Winter
was just one more good intention. The former because that's
what we'd *like* to look like, and the latter because that's
what we're afraid we really *do* look like.

Those who fall into the latter category (and if they
do, they all-too-obviously don't think they do) have not yet
grasped the concept that Spandex is a privilege and not a
right. Back in the days when they actually had the bodies to
carry it off, they wouldn't have been caught dead in clothing
that tight. Somewhere in the intervening years, the fragile
balance between body fat and common sense has tipped
precariously.

They believe that just because the fabric *can* stretch
to quadruple its original width, it *should*.

They are in one of two mind frames. Either they
think that because they own a mountain bike, skintight
sorts are required attire -- a dress code for fat tire enthusi-
asts -- or they buy the mountain bike so they have a valid
excuse to wear the shorts. One often wonders which came
first, and one can usually tell at a single glance at the bike
owner's backside how much use the bike has seen.

Those who wear their lycra-enhanced, one-size-only-
fits-a-chosen-few cycling shorts like a second skin are even
more despicable. They fill us wannabe jocks with a sense of
despair. We know we will never look like that. No one will
ever look like that. They are inhumanly fit and lean and
taut.

(Those of you who saw this particular wannabe
putting her faceprint in the dirt at second base on Sunday,
stop sneering. This is what happens when the muscularly-

challenged delude themselves into thinking they are capable of physical activity.)

There is, of course, another category of Spandex adherents, those who wear a pair of baggy shorts over the Spandex so a mere band of black shows beneath, but the extent of their physical fitness -- unless their chubby knees betray them -- is camouflaged. These people are confused and should be pitied.

Some of you may think I'm taking this concern over elasticity and its relative aesthetic properties (or lack thereof) just a tad too seriously, but I have good cause for my concern.

I just got a mountain bike and, so far, I haven't a thing to wear. And I'm afraid I might have to buy something black and tight.

Is there a dress code for mountain biking???

What this town needs
is a seasonal dress code

December 7, 1993

Christmas can be a very confusing time of year. What to buy, who to buy for, how much to spend, which set of parents is owed the holiday visit this year and at what age do you disabuse your kids of that Santa gravy train?

Here in Canmore, because of the very special nature of our very special community, we face an additional conundrum, one to which our more urban brethren need not give a second thought.

What the heck *does* semi-formal mean in this town, anyway?

Seriously, has anyone out there yet figured out what to wear when the Christmas party invitation arrives bearing those highly ambiguous words? More to the point, has anyone figured out what everyone *else* is wearing when semi-formal is on the agenda?

In the city, or at least in the cities in which I've lived, semi-formal is a dress code, one shade shy of black tie and long gowns. It allows latitude, to be sure, but the standards are such that no woman need spend 15 hours deliberating whether her chosen frock will be too much or too little. Semi-formal is semi-formal, period. Wear something fancy or die of embarrassment.

In Canmore, the greatest wardrobe-friendly town in the world, the concept of semi-formal is infinitely less clear cut, and the invitation to attend a soirée designated semi-formal can be cause for sleepless nights.

For some, a Canmore semi-formal function is a signal to wash and iron one's best blue jeans. For others, it means wearing socks with the track suit. And for still others, it means silk and sequins and a last minute trip to the hairdresser.

Frivolous though it may sound, the receipt of the semi-formal invitation can create for some of us a real dilemma. Is it to be one of those affairs where everyone is so anxious for an opportunity to get out of the jeans that they get gussied to the max, making you feel like the proverbial church mouse when you arrive in denim and flannel?

Worse yet, what if you've completely overestimated the situation and attended in floor-length silk, only to find yourself surrounded by wool sweaters and corduroy?

(Allow me to add a little disclaimer here. While I acknowledge that men are just as prone as women to have anxiety attacks over their attire, they generally manage to escape these potential societal faux pas by possession of at least one jacket, tie and dress shirt and a coordinating pair of slacks. Their major decision seems to revolve around whether a turtleneck will substitute appropriately for the tie and where they're going to put all of their excess gear when you're only carrying a tiny evening bag.)

In a town where the biggest opportunity to play dress-up is the annual fundraiser for the local day care, Christmas should in theory rank a close second on the sartorial scale, but so far what I've seen is everything from hunting caps to diamond bracelets.

I'm confused. What this town really needs (other than lower taxes, slower growth, fewer ravens and better weather) is a seasonal dress code for idiots like me.

ACCESSORY ANGST AND
THE SARTORIALLY DISABLED

July 13, 1994

Some women are born with a fashion sense that gives them the innate ability to coordinate shoes, belts, earrings, nailpolish, lipstick, underwear and scarves without spending an entire month agonizing over the choices.

Others face a recurring dilemma with every purchase made -- to belt or not to belt, that is the question.

This is not a frivolous issue. (No more frivolous than a 24-hour golf channel, to be sure.) Having to attend social functions at which fully accessorized women will be in abundance can create deep-seated angst in some women, leaving emotional scars that hang around longer than mismatched earrings in the bottom of your jewelry box.

I am right now in accessory hell. My presence has been requested at the wedding of my baby brother. Afternoon casual, the invitation said with that glib assumption that *everybody* knows what casual looks like in the context of midday wedding formalities.

It's situations like these that keep me awake nights worried that I'll be either over or underdressed and every other woman there will spend more time whispering about what I wore rather than what the bride wore. I get rather paranoid when separated from my blue jeans.

For me, buying a new dress is like buying a couch and having to build a house around it.

The dress is always the easy part. I tried on two, bought one and happily left with the store owner's reassurance that all I needed were black shoes and a black belt. Oh, and maybe some kind of jewelry that will pick up the purple highlights. Yeah, right. It would be easier for me to figure out the square root of pi than match earrings to fabric.

I own 16 black belts in various widths and textures. Do you think even one of these belts would complement the new frock? Don't be silly.

I own black shoes, too. High heels, low heels, high heeled patent, low heeled leather, high heeled satin Not a single pair that will work with this particular dress. After days of diligent searching I found the perfect pair of flat, patent pumps, but a co-worker in Banff was wearing them at the time and refuses to lend them to me for a week.

The jewelry was a week-long effort. I scoured every shop between here and Lake Louise and finally found myself in an upscale, mall-type Banff boutique where, much to my good fortune, the fully-accessorized sales clerk convinced me that this dress she'd never seen would look much better adorned with a rather tasteful $17 rope of plastic beads cleverly disguised as cheap, fake rocks than with the $250 silver choker I was drooling over. Come to think of it, she probably sized up my denim and sweatshirt attire and decided I'd be in deep doodoo with my bank manager (another accessory-adept woman, I might add) if I went for the choker.

I haven't figured out the pantyhose yet, but I figured I'd buy a pair in every conceivable shade known to womankind and leave that particular agony for the morning of the wedding. Why should the bride have all the fun?

TURNING ONE'S BACK ON
FULL FACE REGALIA

June 29, 1993

The cosmetics industry and I have come to a parting of the ways.

I'm not sure if it's the Canmore lifestyle that has finally planted firm roots in my cranium and convinced me there is nothing more pointless than putting hypo-allergenic, humanely-tested chemical byproducts all over my face just to go to work, or the $14.95 I just spent on an eyeliner pencil.

I've decided it's time for the minimalist look. Actually, I've been gradually working up to it for several months, and now that it's been at least a week since anybody's asked if I was ill, tired or about to faint, I figure you all have gotten used to it. Or are too polite to ask.

I've come full circle, from my 13th birthday when I pleaded, begged and whined for my mother to let me *at least* wear pale pink lipstick to now, when all I carry in my pocket is pale pink lipstick.

Unfortunately, in the 23 intervening years I've left a considerable fraction of my net earnings in cash registers guarded by haughty, white-smocked *Vogue*-ettes who've just graduated from Intimidation 101.

Correct me if I'm wrong, but has not every woman in the western world at one time or another dropped a bundle on items guaranteed to enhance, uplift, depilate and hydrate, not out of necessity but because we were faced with a living, breathing example of what we *too* could look like if we had a little replacement therapy? And did we not heed the implication that there was something wrong with us if *she* was not that to which we aspired?

Exists there a woman who can resist plunking down a few bills for a vial of "unique protective formula containing exclusive EPC-K and Vital-Amino Complex to re-energize skin performance" if it's being proffered by an alabaster-skinned goddess with microscopic pores? (And just how the heck is skin supposed to perform, anyway?)

Who cares if we don't know what this stuff is? Who cares if it sounds like 10W-40 in a pretty package? If *she's* using it, we probably need to, too.

The cosmetics industry has convinced us we're all collagen-deficient and in dire need of daily exfoliation. (I confess I'm a little unclear on this concept. I know defoliation has something to do with clear-cutting forests. Exfoliation sounds like it should have something to do with steel wool.)

In my heart of hearts I know I did not buy a $14.95 easy-glide eyeliner pencil to enhance my appearance. It was because I wanted *her* to think I was merely having a bad face day and had just dashed out to pick up an overpriced but integral part of my daily wardrobe.

There used to be a time when I could wander among those glass counters and comfort myself with the knowledge that I undoubtedly earned far more than those white clad, ephemeral creatures standing guard at the pressed powder and foundation displays. Alas, I fear it's no longer so.

Now that they can call themselves Biomedi/Chemically Trained Color Enhancing Epidermal Aestheticians, I can merely comfort myself with the knowledge that these days it takes me far less time to get ready for work than they.

A NEW VISUAL ACUITY
ENHANCEMENT APPENDAGE

October 29, 1993

Several events this week have conspired to impress upon me that I really am getting old. (None of them had anything to do with that centenarian who celebrated his hundredth birthday by bungee jumping off a crane, a feat I am absolutely certain I will never partake of during my tiny life no matter how decayed my body grows nor how great the temptation to hasten my demise with a self-inflicted heart attack.)

Sign of Aging Number One: I started my Christmas shopping. No greater evidence of maturity have I ever displayed. I'm still pondering the psychological implications of altering life as I know it in the third week of December, when my panic-fueled adrenaline level peaks and my shopping hormones implode with the seasonal frenzy of compulsive consumerism. The possibility looms large that I will actually enjoy this Yuletide instead of stumbling through in a financially and physically exhausted state of depletion.

Sign of Aging Number Two occurred last Wednesday when I raked the leaves in the backyard. Actually, I raked half the leaves in half the backyard, and those three hours of moderate exercise left me completely debilitated for the rest of the week. Could it be my slothful and sedentary lifestyle has finally overtaken my ability to even stretch my arms without causing massive muscle spasms? Is my body trying to tell me something? *(Yo! Lardo! Take me out for a walk!)*

Sign of Aging Number Three, the ultimate evidence of physical decay, was the day I picked up my new spectacles, a rather scholarly-looking pair of wire rims that lend visible and partial credence to any thought you might have had that I'm blind as a bat and dumb as a post. (You're at least half right.)

The first time I realized my father was getting old was the day I saw him don his first pair of reading glasses. I was depressed and saddened. Now here am I, likewise dependent on corrective lenses not only to read but to drive a car, watch television and even to determine what's in the back of the refrigerator.

At least the transformation of my appearance wasn't as drastic as I'd feared. A colleague at work peered at me for several moments, puzzled, before asking if I'd changed my hairstyle. On Friday I covered a public meeting jammed with people who are abundantly familiar with my face at these functions. Not a word was said. On Saturday I had coffee for 45 minutes with a friend who's known me for 15 years. He didn't notice.

All in all, the transformation has been positive. Old though I feel, in six short days I have gone from a world where everything had fuzzy edges to one with clarity and focus. Literally speaking, of course.

Would that the same could be said for life in general and politics in particular.

WHEN FASHION BECOMES
A BATTLEGROUND

September 21, 1993

For years my slightly-older sister talked about getting her nose pierced. Long before it became a trendoid thing to do, long before Birkenstocks replaced earth shoes and grunge surpassed Polo shirts, she talked about Having It Done.

I'm not sure what held her back, whether it was the fear of pain, the fear of standing out too much in a crowd (although to my way of thinking this seemed the only real reason for Having It Done in the first place) or the paucity of neighborhood nose-piercers, but she hasn't mentioned it much lately. I suspect that now that she's reached the age of slightly-older-than-me she's abandoned the idea.

I mention this because very recently her daughter turned 13 and the big question on my mind is what my slightly-older sister is going to do when her offspring wants to pierce her own nose or tattoo a third eye in the centre of her forehead.

So far, my niece seems a happy, well-adjusted, bright and entertaining young woman, but I know from my own experience as a hideous teenager that this is merely a phase she's going through. She's lulling us into a false sense of serenity over how well she's turned out. Any week now she's going to emerge from her bedroom with black nailpolish and a *Chocolate Bunnies from Hell* T-shirt and she and my sister will no longer have to worry about borrowing each other's clothes.

I swore when I was a teenager I was never going to turn into one of those grownups who become so entrenched in middle age that they forget what youth is all about and look down on everything that is rad, cool, gnarly or otherwise emblematic of adolescence.

And I'm not. I have no problem whatsoever with the state of teenage fashion. In fact, I get kind of a nostalgic kick out of the new uniform of baggy shirts, oversized jeans sliding off their butts, pant legs wide enough to drive a her of cattle through and clunky black Doc Martens.

(Flashback to 1972: peasant blouses, platform shoes and baggy bell bottoms slung low enough on the hips to drive a herd of, well, you know.)

On the surface it all screams nonconformity, but on closer inspection one realizes they all want to look alike. It's *us* they don't want to look like.

Fair enough. It's all part of the adolescent experience of forging one's own distinct identity away from the parental units. Plus it will give *us* some pretty hilarious pictures to look at 20 years from now while *they* howl with laughter at how stupidly their parents dressed in the old days.

It also explains something about which I've often wondered, and that is why otherwise right-thinking adults spend so much time, effort and money dressing their infant children in the latest fashions, complete with tiny ties, blazers and, for girls, little lace garters stretched around their little bald heads. I mean, the little darlings are just going to drool all over everything anyway, so why bother, right?

Wrong. It's the one window of opportunity parents have in a lifetime of arguing over their offspring's attire where they have complete control over what their children will wear.

Fashion Advice for
The Confused Male

November 24, 1992

It must be tough to be a Nineties kinda guy. Even without the minor issues one confronts regularly -- to buy or to rent, a Ford or a Jeep, cable or satellite -- one is faced with a myriad of dilemmas one's fathers and grandfathers never even imagined would one day be crucial.

Who pays for the first date? Should you let her beat you at pool? Who stays home with the baby for the first year? Do you need a home computer? A Mac or IBM? Which cellular phone offers the best bang for its buck? Will the laserdisc system be obsolete by next February?

And, of course, the absolute biggie -- to pierce or not to pierce? Ah yes, that is the question, isn't it?

A lot of guys are faced with this conundrum these days, judging by the number of earrings dangling incongruously from totally inappropriate earlobes.

At one time, a man wearing an earring symbolized to the world that he was daring, a non-conformist, a totally cool dude. Nowadays, however, it has become such an ubiquitous fashion statement that not only is it in danger of losing its appeal, its statement is quickly becoming one of: "I am a sheep and a slave to the passing whims of fashion. And I have no idea what I look like in the mirror."

Hey guys, let's face it. Earrings are to men what red lipstick is to women. Some people just shouldn't do it.

Nine-year-old boys should definitely not do it. No boy should be allowed to pierce any body part pre-puberty. It just makes them look geeky. In fact, no one of the male species should be allowed to pierce their ears before they can grow facial hair. One without the other just doesn't cut it.

Hyper-macho studly kind of guys should definitely not do it, especially if they're trying to accessorize an enormous beer belly and jeans that ride halfway down their butts. If you want to make a fashion statement, clean your fingernails.

Guys who wear their hair in a purple mohawk and already have three diamond studs in their left nostril shouldn't do it. What's the point?

Guys who wear suits and get their hair cut at the same place as the local constabulary shouldn't do it. Even though the misuse of the male earring has removed most of its impact, if you're going to dress like a corporate cookie cutter the earring's going to clash. Badly.

Guys who wear uniforms really shouldn't wear their ear gear until they're off duty. This applies to cops, soldiers, firefighters, gas station attendants, bus drivers and paramedics. Chefs and bakers have some leeway.

Guys born before 1947 should not do it, unless of course you had yours done in 1977 when it was still avante garde. If you're a grandfather, however, you might want to reconsider.

Guys who wear ponytails can do it, but only if the ponytail is longer than the rubber band holding it in place and only until the ponytail reaches the kind of mass conformity the earring has. Then you'll have to find something different.

And cowboys should never, ever wear earrings.

THE GLOVED AND MARTINI
CROWD MAKES A RETURN

November 1, 1994

The little black dress is making a comeback. So is the dry martini. Miniskirts are definitely in for evening wear, and long black gloves are enjoying a resurgence in popularity, depending of course on circumstance and availability. Red lipstick is still the color of choice for evening wear, regardless of one's skin pallor, and faux diamonds are back on the earlobes.

For anyone paralyzed by indecision as they ponder their choices for the weekly foray to the corner tavern -- you're welcome. Just think of my as your little local fashion consultant.

Actually, I know all of this for two reasons. Firstly, *Chatelaine* magazine says this is all so in its latest edition, and if it's good enough for Hogtown you just know it will filter back to the boonies in short order. And secondly, I had to do the socializing thing this past week and can attest to the fact that it already has filtered back to the boonies.

It was purely a work function, *sans* spouses, and much to my amazement many of the other attendees at this two-day affair opted to dress to the nines for a cocktail hour in a real Banff bar and dinner back in the same seminar room in which we'd already spent six hours.

Except for the Canmore people, of course. We kept our Birkenstocks and denims on, and wore them with pride.

(An editorial disclaimer here, before anyone pounces on me for being a clothing snob. I acknowledge the fact that for some people, dressing up is something in which they take great pleasure. Yesterday was Hallowe'en and we all saw ample evidence of this. What I'm saying is, I'm mystified by it all. If it's not Christmas, why bother?)

Irony of ironies, I own all of that stuff. Little black dresses, fake diamond drops, yes, even the long black gloves, presented as a gift from a dear friend who knew I would fall over laughing at their inclusion in my wardrobe. Yes, I have worn them. In public.

I've even done the martini thing, back in my uptown kinda days, and learned quickly it's not the kind of drink one can consume recreationally in a public establishment and expect to get through the evening with any kind of decorum. Apparently this is still so.

Is it just me, or are these fashion cycles starting to spin a lot more rapidly? Or is that the sound of my own personal calendar hitting fast forward? It was barely 10 years ago the black dress/gloves/martini were symbolic of sophistication and success, and suddenly they are back on the scene.

Does this mean the recession is officially over and we are returning again to the excesses of the Eighties, or merely that the fashion dragoons have rediscovered LSD and forgotten which fashion they were supposed to resurrect for this season?

Maybe it means we can all take heart and quit chucking clothes. Guys, hang onto those Flintstone ties. At this rate, they'll be back in style by May.

SECTION FOUR
ECCENTRICITY IS A RELATIVE CONCEPT

CHILDREN, DO YOU KNOW
WHERE YOUR PARENTS ARE?

February 8, 1994

There comes a time in every child's life when one must confront an obvious and inescapable truth.

Your parents are people, too.

Usually this becomes evident somewhere in your teens, when the realization dawns that Buddy Holly and Elvis would have been your parents' contemporaries. Your mother probably owned a poodle skirt and saddle shoes and spent too much time on the phone with her girlfriends. Your father no doubt dwelled under the hood of a '54 Chevy and the two of them, once they started dating, probably spent a few evenings parked in a steamy car down some back lane.

(My mother, however, denies to this day any such impropriety, leaving me with a lingering belief in Immaculate Conception that outlived by 15 years my belief in Santa Claus.)

Until you yourself acknowledge adulthood, parents are merely there for your convenience. The concept of them having walked the same road to maturity is a foreign to you as the 20-foot snowdrifts they walked through to school. Their childhood, if such a thing ever occurred, pre-dated the Stone Age and the one phrase you shudder to hear come out of their mouths is "When I was your age..."

Somehow we all come through it, and as adults hopefully learn to appreciate and enjoy parents for the experienced, wise and intelligent people they are. Rational political discussions and pleasant reminiscing replace hormonally-driven eruptions around the dinner table, and a phone call from the folks is no longer interpreted as lack of trust.

My parents are just now entering their 60s, reasonably healthy, prematurely retired and financially secure enough to adopt a relatively carefree existence of summers at the cottage and several months of winter travel. Every year, shortly after Christmas, they pile all of their prescription medications and the cat into a slightly beat up old Winnebago and head out for warmer parts unknown, a couple of greying vagabonds with golf clubs.

Not quite Dennis Hopper and Peter Fonda, but I'm sure in their minds there's a parallel.

And each year, at about this time, my misspent, inconsiderate, self-centered adolescence comes back to haunt me. My parents never, ever, think to call home.

They've been gone for four weeks now, and I'm getting a little antsy. The last time I heard from them was on Day One, when they called to say they'd been broadsided by a drunk driver and had engine trouble somewhere in North Dakota. (Which was not the purpose of the phone call. They called to say they realized they'd forgotten to tell me they were leaving for a few months and they thought I might worry. What, me worry??)

I have a general idea of their itinerary, insofar as it includes Nevada and Arizona. Beyond that I have not a clue. We are ostensibly a closely knit family, but when they get to having fun, sometimes they forget the time. And the month.

The next time I will hear from them will be sometime in mid-March when they call to tell me to get the spare bedroom ready for their arrival on their way back through Alberta. Until then, I try not to get too worried about all of the dangers lurking out there that could befall a couple of old teenagers just out for a good time.

HOW TO TELL WHEN YOU'RE

FINALLY A GROWN UP

March 22, 1994

Every once in a while, when the increasingly common *Warning: This Movie is For Mature Audiences Only* flashes

across the TV at the outset of whatever banality Hollywood
has chosen for my viewing pleasure that evening, I am left
wondering.

Do I qualify?

What is maturity, anyway? Is it purely advanced age,
as the movie makers would have us believe, or is it a state of
mind?

Should not the warning read: *For Immature Audiences Only,* if one is going to devote an entire two hours to
watching Jean Claude Van Damme kick in bad guys' faces,
toss his ponytail and flash his well-oiled pecs in numerous
bimbos' beds? Is devoting more than 30 seconds to such pap
a mature thing to do?

Are Thirtysomething editors still hooked on a weekly
fix of Bugs Bunny mature enough to watch violence made
sexy and sex made violent?

Years alone cannot be used as a measure of maturity.
Some teenagers are more than capable of watching suppos-
edly adult movies and reading adult books without having
their psyches warped. Some adults I know are still not
mature enough to read adult books.

Chronologically speaking, I suppose I am mature. In
doggie years I am slightly over five and well past the puppy
chow stage. I can tie my own shoes and cross the street
alone, but balancing a cheque book and investing wisely are
skills which elude me, though I have always associated them
with maturity.

Mature adults save carefully, budget wisely and plan
ahead when taking a vacation. They research their destination, calculate their daily itineraries and even think to
cancel the newspapers. Others get their income tax rebates
and are on the next plane to Florida.

Mature? Perhaps not, but is spontaneity necessarily
an immature trait? Does being more carefree and less encum-
bered by debt delineate immaturity, or merely the choice of
Disney World as a holiday destination?

Having children is supposed to make people mature,
but some of the best parents I've ever known are those who
retain their ability to play with the pure joy of children,
those who can maintain the same prone position for several

hours while examining an ant hill, and who think allowances *should* be spent on jawbreakers and pogs. Are these mature individuals? Should they not be doing laundry or something?

Buying a house is an extremely mature thing to do, I've always thought, unless of course one is overextending oneself for the sake of a status address, which is very immature indeed and completely eliminates any possibility of a spontaneous flight to Florida in exchange for the shallow admiration of those who equate wealth with respect.

Unlike savings bonds and mutual funds, we humans do not hit a certain expiry date at which we are deemed mature. We are somehow supposed to know all by ourselves when we reach this magical milestone, but the parameters are vague and shifting.

There really is only one true measure of maturity. When you finally learn to make your own decisions without consulting your parents, but consult them anyway because *you* know *they* know more than you, you're probably mature.

There's a special place in heaven for Aunties

August 11, 1992

When I was much younger, a chief source of amusement was making life miserable for my kid brother. A day would not have been complete had I not sent him screaming to mother for his regular reminder: "Just wait until you get older"

He's older now, and he's evened the score big time. He made me an Auntie, three times over, even enlisting my complicity by naming his eldest Christine Carol and ensuring an eternal soft spot in my heart for a four-year-old who

just left hot dog buns ground into my carpet and the cry of
"Why-y-y ?" echoing in my ears.

There must be a special place in heaven for Aunties.
If there isn't, there should be. Aunties without children of
their own go to the head of the line.

When people have children there is theoretically
some measure of choice involved. When, how many, how
many years apart and, for the lucky ones, the big Whether.
Aunties have no such choice. A sibling's opinion in family
planning is rarely taken into account.

Once you become an Auntie, your only option is to
stake out a relationship with them that is either adult
disciplinarian or benign piggy-back provider. When one of
those offspring bears your name, you have no choice.

They descended (for lack of a better word) on Friday
at 4 p.m. and departed Saturday night, leaving in their wake
half a pitcher of purple Kool-Aid somehow overlooked, a
fridge covered with carefully scrawled crayon masterpieces
and a sucking vortex of silence to which I'm still trying to
adjust.

Along with the aforementioned Christine Carol came
three-year-old Ricky (who also answers to Bucko or Icky,
depending on who's calling and what their mood is) and
year-old toddler Brittani, still trying to master the intricacies
of this thing we call walking.

I'd anticipated their visit with the kind of selective
memory loss that lets women go through childbirth more
than once. Five minutes after their arrival I was listening to
*"Auntie, tell Brittani not to put her hand in the toilet when
I'm going poo!"* emanate from the bathroom and wondering
just what it was my maternal instincts had been missing so
much.

My brother went golfing with a friend, who donated
his dog to the general melee, an unplanned gesture of
generosity that shall not go unrewarded. The dog promptly
licked Brittani's face and sent her howling to the protection
of her Mommy, a woman who will forever be known to me
as Saint Kathy. For revenge, Brittani later upended the dog's
water dish all over herself and the carpet.

Ricky spent the day feeding the dog peanut butter cookies and trying to determine if its eyes were real, while Auntie tried to answer thousands of questions from a four-year-old that all started with the word "Why?" This is how I found myself sitting in my own kitchen at 11 p.m. on a Saturday night explaining the workings of a corkscrew to a pre-schooler.

We went to the playground and had a picnic and fed the ducks and watched E.T. four times, all things guaranteed to make a visit with Auntie memorable in years to come. Brittani removed all the spaghetti from an open box in the cupboard, Ricky pulled the batik from the wall and Christine took home all the rocks from the neighbor's flower garden, all things guaranteed to ensure Auntie never forgets, either.

Nor will she easily forget the sight of tiny arms upstretched from knee level for hugs that needed no reason and the silky blond hair on the head of a sturdy little deadweight boy who'd fallen asleep in her lap.

As they were leaving Saint Kathy apologized for the brevity of the visit, promising to stay longer next time. I'm not sure, but I think I can hardly wait.

'TIS THE SEASON TO GET A VALIUM PRESCRIPTION

November 10, 1992

I've been having a recurring nightmare lately. I'm back in my parents' living room in Saskatoon, surrounded by my siblings and their offspring. Bing Crosby's crooning *Winter Wonderland* on the stereo and the children are playing at our feet as we sit quietly talking, bathed in the light of the crackling fire and the intermittent flashing of the Christmas tree lights.

Bing Crosby... the Christmas tree lights... the Christmas tree lights...

Oh my God! (Insert mental image of MacAulay Culkin as he realizes he's *Home Alone*) I've forgotten to buy Christmas presents!

I awake in a panic of shame and cold sweat. Hallowe'en's over and I have just six weeks and three paycheques left. Time to get shopping. Wrapping. Writing. Mailing. Baking. Ack!

I hate this time of year. I love Christmas, I just hate the lead time. It gives me no consolation to know every other person alive feels the same stress and pressure. It just means we're *all* going to be cranky for the next two months.

TV commercials are starting to flog Barbie's Mega-Million Mansion and magazine racks are sprouting special seasonal publications like *Make Christmas Easy and Elegant* with Do-It-All Weekly Planners, containing such handy tips as when to enroll in a crafts class (Nov. 15) to make your own quilted centrepiece. Yeah, right.

Once again my family has decided to "only buy for the children", and once again I know everyone is going to cheat and buy for everyone else on the assumption than everyone else is cheating too, and it would just be too humiliating to arrive less than fully-armed with gifts for all. We are so trusting.

Once again I will make lists and calculate prices and check catalogues. Then I will shred the lists and abandon any notion ever harbored about fiscal responsibility and plunge headlong into Toys 'R' Us like I'm on some maniacal search and destroy mission. (This is not a woman who enjoys utilitarian shopping. You've seen how I dress.)

I will buy boxes of cards and buckets of stamps and with luck I will write a grand total of 16 Yuletide greetings to be mailed in February. I will assemble all of the ingredients to make antipasto and elegant hors d'oeuvres, and all of the fancy jars, tins and baskets in which to package them for last minute, unexpected dinner invitations. It will all sit in my cupboards until next summer, when I might have time to cook.

Just once I would like to have the kind of Christmas the people in these magazines have, with time to make my own garlands and wreaths with which to decorate the house, with time to curl up by the fire and re-read *A Christmas Carol*. I would like the time to write individual, lengthy notes to be enclosed in the mailed-on-time Christmas cards, with time to shop for a little black dress to wear to *The Nutcracker*, with time to make mincemeat and shortbread and Cranberry Nut Loaf for those impromptu get togethers after an afternoon spent building an entire nativity scene out of snow in the front yard...

Ho ho ho. Who *are* these people, anyway?

THE CAT GETS LUCKY,
THE FOLKS GET RICH

January 24, 1995

A cat is stealing my inheritance.

A small, fluffy, haughty pedigreed bundle of hostility has supplanted me in the family hierarchy. She's cute, she's tattooed and she's in heat, and my parents are spending *way* too much money to ensure she gets pregnant.

The folks have become animal elitists. After decades of filling the family home with an eclectic assortment of white rats, scruffy cats and genetically dubious dogs, they have embraced the concept of a superior race and bought an ultra-expensive feline with an attitude problem.

You know that commercial for the cat food that comes in caviar-sized cans and is served in a crystal sherbet glass to a pug-nosed, long-haired white cat named Princess or Jeeves or some such nonsense?

It's that kind of cat and yes, they feed it that kind of cat food. In plain white china saucers.

Last night my mother called to update me on the insemination campaign. (Discussions of the cat's sex life have become all too commonplace around the dinner table, leaving the human offspring with a vague sense of disquiet, wondering whether we, too, have been similarly dissected and our breeding potential so cavalierly pondered. We are also secretly relieved that our mates did not have to undergo the same kind of genetic scrutiny to produce grandchildren that Suki's list of potential suitors has had to endure.)

After months and months of searching, they've found a "stud" for Suki, Mother excitedly announced. (Somehow "stud" and "cat" don't seem to fit in the same sentence, do they?) Suki was spending her first night alone with her new beau, Mother said, describing in great detail the "conversation" the two had upon introduction.

I listened with bemusement, pondering the true impact of the empty nest syndrome on a woman who doesn't have access to her grandchildren on a 24-hour a day basis, when she casually dropped into the conversation the price they were paying for a few million of Mr. Studly's spermatozoa.

Whoa! Hold the fort! We're not talking chump change, here. If I tried to borrow that from my father, he'd made me sign papers, but here he is signing cheques for his cat to have a few hours of fun and frolic?!?

I have known other people who devote their lives to raising purebreds of one species or another, be it dogs or birds or tropical fish. I've never really understood the fascination, other than that all-too human desire to own something rare, but live and let live, eh?

Except when it's your own parents spending huge, unmanageable amounts of cash on a creature that could be coyote fodder at any minute. Then, you really start to question the wisdom and sanity of genetic engineering in the animal kingdom.

Before I had a chance to give vocal vent to my indignation, Mother told me what Ms. Suki's offspring, should Mr. Studly succeed, would fetch on the common market, and I realize I've got it all wrong. Should there be kittens, they would each be more valuable than the entire net worth of my personal stock portfolio.

With luck, one of those little furballs will *be* my inheritance.

So what do you do with 20lbs. of leftovers?

October 13, 1992

The burning question today is not who to vote for in next Monday's municipal election. It's not which way to vote on Oct. 26, and it's not whether Them Jays are actually going to win the pennant.

It's what to do with the leftovers. Yes, *those* leftovers.

I'm about to do something I've never done before. Shamelessly plead for help. I need suggestions. I need advice. I need recipes. I have a serious, major, monumental-type poultry problem on my hands.

I bought a 27-pound turkey for Thanksgiving this year. It wasn't my idea, but by the time late Saturday afternoon rolled around and I got around to picking up the fresh, previously-ordered bird destined to feed 12 people, all that was left was Godzilla's younger brother. No time to thaw a frozen one for Sunday's repast, no time to shop around at another store in another town or even another province for one even slightly less substantial. (Fellow procrastinators, take note. This could happen to *you* someday.)

Roasting a turkey this large requires some serious logistical considerations. There isn't a roasting pan known to mankind that will hold it, nor an oven rack sturdy enough to support it without developing a serious bow in the middle. I know. Think aluminium foil. Think yards and yards and yards of aluminum foil. You get the picture.

I made 20 cups of stuffing Saturday night, and another 20 cups at 5 a.m. Sunday when it didn't even fill *half* the cavity. It went in the oven at 8 a.m. and came out at 7 p.m., picture perfect and just in time to stave off hunger-induced hysteria. It didn't shrink, as I'd hoped.

We carved an entire quarter of it and fed the dozen easily. It's the other three quarters and two drumsticks I'm having a problem with.

The family came, the family ate, the family departed for distant parts -- leftoverless.

So what do you do with them? Don't suggest soup, please. The newly acquired 20 quart stock pot is, as we speak, simmering with a carcass roughly the size of my three year old nephew. I will be eating turkey soup for a very long time to come.

The season dictates that there will be a limited market of friends and acquaintances upon whom I can pawn off cooked turkey. They have their own disposal problems. A few of my colleagues who did not cook their own will gratefully accept free turkey sandwiches for just so many days before I have a serious revolt on my hands.

I may suck in a few close friends on the pretext of having an impromptu dinner party and try to tart it up as turkey lasagna and turkey casserole. I might run out of friends.

And what the devil am I going to do with the five-pound turkey neck in my freezer that couldn't fit in the oven with the rest of Big Bird?

Seriously folks, I'm asking for help. I have a limited imagination when it comes to such things.

Vegetarians appalled at this crass lack of sensitivity on my part, please restrain yourselves from calling to chastise me for my carnivorous habits.

I am about to join your ranks.

Don't get mad. Get even.
Even with your mother.

February 23, 1993

Somebody asked me recently where I get my ideas for this column. It's very simple, really.

Desperation. Sunday night hysteria-driven creativity spawned by a vast expanse of white space that will either be filled with Chamber of Commerce news releases or whatever I can dredge out of my slightly-bent imagination.

Plus it helps that I come from an extremely weird family. (Actually, only my mother's side of the family carried the extra chromosome. Father and his kin were fairly normal, but the maternal branch was a different breed.)

We were sort of the Addams Family of Winnipeg's East Kildonan, outwardly acceptable enough to avoid visits by Children's Aid but privately dedicated to making each others' adrenal glands function in perpetual overdrive.

We didn't actually use explosives or anything like that -- although for years, unknown to the rest of us, my youngest brother stored the fuel for his model rockets under his bed, a practise that only came to light when he felt beholden to caution a visiting uncle against smoking in that particular bed.

No, we were more the water buckets and cream pie kind of family, a collection of eccentrics who learned from a very young age to watch your back, cover your butt and check your shoes before putting them on.

One of my earliest childhood memories is of lying on the upper bunk of a TeePee trailer camped by a lakeside in B.C., listening to my mother and *her* mother laughing hysterically as they frantically scrambled up from the beach with their arms full of clothes, pursued by my buck naked and bellowing grandfather who'd been caught skinny dipping.

(In later years I learned that *any* opportunity to get even with Grandpa was one to be seized. I spent my thirteenth birthday huddled behind an upturned dining room table, playing trench warfare with little spit balls of plasticine fired from that same grandfather barricaded behind the sofa. It was he who taught us all we know about flipping dishtowels to maximize welts, how to put a frozen minnow in a snorer's mother without awakening them and how to cheat at cribbage.)

Our water fights were monumental, ranging over entire city blocks and once, as I recall, ending in the police being summoned to a complaint of a screaming teenage girl being chased by a man on a motorcycle, armed with a bucket.

So I shouldn't have been that surprised last week when I discovered my mother had snuck that perfectly *wretched* photo of me into my own newspaper and announced to all and sundry that yes, my little lifetime odometer has clicked another mile.

I can't get even right away. Dad's taken her to some unknown parts of the U.S. for some little rest and rehab. Guess she'd started forgetting the names of family members again. She's at that age.

But get even I will. I must stop her before she rhymes again. And Mom, if you're reading this -- and I know you are -- there was one little flaw in the plan.

Never pick a fight with a reporter. They *always* have the last word.

A FEW SHORT WORDS ON
HEIGHT DEFICIENCIES

May 5, 1992

Not too long ago, at one of those semi-social functions I attend periodically as both guest and local editor, I encountered a situation for which Miss Manners has failed to prepare me.

A gentleman of -- I'm guessing, and if he's offended he deserves to be -- my father's age passed me in a crowded aisle and momentarily rested his chin upon my head.

"I just wanted to see if I could," he said, and slipped on into the crowd.

I was a little taken aback. Would he have done this if I were older? Probably not. Would he have done this if I were male? Doubtful. Would he have done this if I were taller? Definitely not.

I am short. Vertically challenged.

I have lived with this condition all of my life. It is incurable and occasionally as debilitating as left-handedness. The world as we know it is built for, and by, people who conform to a standard. Everything on the right, and everything at a height.

In my gene pool, I am a throwback.

Daily I am reminded of my shortcomings. In the IGA, I have to scale the upright shelving to reach the mineral water on the top shelves. In the corner grocery, I can only stare at the magazine titles so neatly lined up at the rear on the top.

I avoid furniture. In your living room I would opt for the floor because to sit on the couch would leave my feet sticking out horizontally like a small child's.

Don't talk to me about cars. Cars are designed and built by men with a six-foot-four mentality. Even if the seat does go forward enough to allow my feet contact with the pedals I am still forced to view the world through the spokes of a steering wheel.

House builders discriminate, too. The average abode is constructed to a standard that is well above, if you'll pardon the expression, what I require. For years, until well-meaning friends bought me my first stepladder, I was deprived of the use of top closet and cupboard shelves.

Small children use me as a measuring stick once they reach the age of, oh, seven, by which time they are usually about up to my shoulder and already well-versed in the equation that bigger is better.

Even the word carries negative connotations. Short changed. Short tempered. Short handed. Short sighted. The dictionary defines the word as "having little linear extension; deficient; inadequate."

If a person is successful, they are head and shoulders above the crowd." A failure "falls short of the mark." A tall, successful person is "Lincolnesque". A short succeeder has a Napoleonic complex

I cannot rise to an occasion. Everything goes over my head. I can stand up and be counted, but who'd notice.

And the worst of all? I can grow old, but I can never grow up.

How to talk like a Mom

Something strange and mysterious happens to women when they become mothers. (Other than magically sprouting eyes in the back of their heads, I mean.)

They acquire a whole new language, one that has survived through the years in somewhat the same way as cherished recipes, passed from generation to generation in a time-honored ritual so loaded with emotional apron strings that it's a wonder the female of the species is still willing to do that reproduction thing.

Somewhere between infancy's "Oooh! Did da wittle fella get enough nummies in his tummy?" and adolescence's "I hope when you have children they turn out just like you!" comes an entire, complicated phraseology that encompasses every conceivable sin a son or daughter may commit -- or consider. Such is Motherhood.

The language has, in all likelihood, evolved considerably. "If all your friends wanted to jump off a bridge would you want to, too?" probably started out as, "If all your friends wanted to jump off the parthenon, would you want to, too?"

Don't you just want to bet that Cleopatra's mother, at some point in her daughter's young life, ordered her back to her chambers to scrub off that eye makeup? And that Joan of Arc's Mom tried to get her daughter to act more like a lady?

Want to know why God is really a woman? Who was it told Eve -- "Don't eat that!" (What the Bible doesn't record is that the whole sentence was likely --"Don't eat that, it's for lunches!")

Did Mona Lisa's Mother say, "Wipe that smirk off your face"?

Did Liz Taylor's Mother tell her, "It's just as easy to fall in love with a rich man as a poor man"?

Parenting has experienced many changes through the ages, but even Attila the Hun's Mother was likely overheard to say: "Just wait until your father gets home".

Pick up your feet. Pick up your toys. It's good for you.

You're not leaving the table until it's all gone. Why didn't you go before we left the house? I'll think about it. Ask your father. Stop running with that, you'll put your eye out. I mean it. Stop it or I'm taking you home right now. What do you mean, there's nothing to do? It's a beautiful day outside, turn off that TV. Don't sit so close to the TV, you'll ruin your eyes. Turn on a light to read that, you'll ruin your eyes.

I just don't want you to make the same mistakes I did. You're too young. You're too old. Wear your boots. I don't care what the other Moms let them do. I'm not the other Moms.

And the big whopper -- "Because I'm the Mom, that's why".

You who are childless may laugh now, but the very act of childbirth apparently mutates your vocabulary. You can swear on a stack of prayer books that your children will never be subjected to such language, until you find yourself late at night with a four-year-old who refuses to stay in bed and you hear yourself shouting, "If I have to come up there one more time..."

Section five
It's an odd, odd, odd, odd, odd, odd world

THEY GET BOBBITT,
WE GET SNOW AND MOSQUITOES

January 18, 1994

Isn't it just so Canadian that in the same week the U.S. media is churning out endless stories of violence and mayhem in the genteel world of figure skating and updating hourly the length of John Bobbitt's manhood, all we could muster for our nightly newscasts was the weather.

Stop the presses! News flash! It's cold in Canada in January!

Good grief.

They get Heidi Fleiss and Michael Jackson, we get late-breaking items on the elimination of our MPs' parliamentary shoe shine privileges. Is this fair?

Here we are, trapped in the icy hinterlands of our now vertically-realigned continent, and we're stuck with newspapers that still actually cover the war in Bosnia.

We get a Prime Ministers who reads books and understands art, they get a president whose alleged sexual indiscretions bump Burt and Loni out of the tabloids.

Their wild card politician is a Texas billionaire who claims Libyan death plots against him and electronically spies on his own employees. We get an Alberta consultant in a grey flannel suit.

They have Marla and la Donald to titillate their interest in the rich and famous. The Trumps buy casinos. They get engaged and break up and then have a baby and get married abruptly after a gunman goes berserk on a New York commuter train.

We get Barbara Amiel and Conrad Black. He has anxiety attacks.

They get earthquakes, hurricanes and floods and have officially-declared states of emergency. We get snow and mosquitoes, neither of which qualify for federal funding.

They get all the best Elvis sightings, too, and now they're laying claim to Sasquatch. Where will it end? Does the wholesale export of our water down south mean Ogopogo will one day end up in one of their lakes, too?

One wonders whether, once the full effects of NAFTA are felt, will be Canadians actually have a home grown steady diet of the kind of useless, trivial, voyeuristic information that apparently sells newspapers and improves ratings.

(Mike Cardinal doesn't count. Mike Cardinal and the out-of-wedlock child he fathered and neglected to fund were a legit story. I don't care what Ted Byfield says. If Mike Cardinal were a pinko socialist, Ted Byfield's opinion of whether he should be forgiven and excused would be 180 degrees different.)

Under NAFTA, will our organs of communication (forget Bobbitt for a minute, we're talking about newspapers here) be up for grabs by American conglomerates more concerned with ratings and numbers than content and fairness?

(I know this latter statement could be applied to Ralph Klein's little fireside chat last night, but that's an accidental analogy.)

Will the Sony Corporation turn its yen-filled wallets north and see profits to be made in the exploitation of the elk rutting season? Will backers of the kind of chequebook journalism practiced by *Inside Edition* and *Hard Copy* set up shop north of 49? Will Rupert Murdoch buy the *Canmore Leader*?

Probably not. We Canadians just can't seem to generate the kind of cash-fueled news copy that interests them. Maybe if we continue to practice Boring as a Lifestyle we'll escape their attention altogether. We can only hope.

Never underestimate
the Goddess of Irony

January 12, 1993

One of the more amusing gifts I got for Christmas this year
was a Murphy's Law calendar, one of those handy little desk
jobbies that feeds you a cute little quip for every day of the
year, along the lines of "Whatever can go wrong will go
wrong" and "In order to get a loan you must first prove you
don't need it."

Murphy's good, no doubt about it, but he's not as
good as the power that propels my tiny life into its more
hideous moments. Years ago, several women friends and I
acknowledged this exclusively female force and bestowed
upon her the noble title of The Goddess of Irony.

There isn't a woman alive who hasn't had at least
one encounter with the Goddess, because the Goddess only
works on women. We're not sure if she's married or if there
even is a God of Irony, but she does seem to work in tandem
with the comparatively benign Murphy.

Unfortunately, she manifests some purely female
traits that Murphy can't use in his calendars because guys
wouldn't be able to relate.

For example, the Goddess of Irony is the force that
dictates your period will be late the same day the landlord
calls to say your rent cheque's bounced.

The Goddess says that when you lose weight, you
will lose it from your breasts first.

The Goddess ensures that when you're wearing your
grubbiest jeans and grungiest sweatshirt, upon which you've
just spilled something, you will bump into the gorgeous man
you exchanged phone numbers with the week before, or an
old boyfriend you haven't seen in seven years with his
incredibly beautiful new wife who is wearing a perfectly
tailored Sung suit.

The Goddess arranges things so that when your car
blows a tire it will be right in front of a crew of hugely-

muscled highway workers who will ignore your plight in the mistaken assumption that you're trying to prove something by changing it yourself.

She also gives your car PMS as soon as you have an extra $100 in the chequing account.

The Goddess fluctuates your estrogen levels at whim, generally elevating them to perfectly coincide with the one particular day of the month in which it is absolutely imperative that you have a zit-free face. The Goddess will also ensure you're retaining water when the aforementioned gorgeous guy finally calls and invites you over for a hot tub.

When you're sitting in a stall in a public washroom, gossiping with your friend in the next stall, the Goddess will compel the subject of your gossip to quietly enter and fix her lipstick.

The Goddess works with the Fashion Gods to make sure that as soon as you finally decide to purge the platform shoes, crocheted vests and peace symbol earrings from your closet, they will all come back into style and sell for astronomically high prices at the vintage clothing store. Likewise, as soon as you summon up the courage to buy and wear a mini skirt, hemlines will plunge.

The Goddess' most ironic work, however, is done on the aging process. As you grow older, you will become more and more like your mother. And when you have children, they will be as your mother threatened -- Just Like You.

WE NEED A LAW AGAINST
OVER-UTILIZATION OF WORDS

March 23, 1993

I got a letter from a lawyer last week. It took me three and a half hours to get past the first sentence. Ninety-six counts of "hereby", three "in consideration ofs", one "releasor", two "releasees" and 107 commas.

Now, all you lawyers in town, don't jump on me for what I'm about to say. This is in no way an attack on your professionalism or personal integrity or anything like that, but I've got a problem with the way you folks talk. Not your personal conversations, I hasten to add. I've never had a personal conversation with a lawyer I couldn't understand -- except for that one fine gentleman who complains that we never report his ski race wins at the Nordic Centre but we always put his name in the paper when he loses a case in court, but that's another story. I digress.

It's the legal language you employ that has me confused. I almost had to hire another lawyer just to interpret my letter for me.

If this kind of grammatical stunting was limited to the legal profession I could probably ignore it, but the word *utilize* is spreading to the rest of the population and I hold you all responsible.

Lawyers become politicians who hire consultants who hire public relations spokespeople who try to explain the government to us plebes and end up saying things like "We realize there has been a significant postal flow on this issue" when what they really mean to say is "A whole bunch of people are mad at us and they are writing us letters."

Check this out, from the recently-released Tourism Association of Alberta marketing strategy: "The proximity of the Alberta and Regional markets also allow them to generate significant numbers of same day person-trips: a trip type not often generated by visitors from markets further away from Alberta."

Now what the heck is a "person-trip" and where does it get you?

Believe it or not, this pseudo-intellectual is stating the obvious. People who live in or near Alberta are more likely to holiday in Alberta than people who live farther away. No kidding. Maybe they figured if they tarted up the words they could more easily justify the consultant's price tag.

Here's another of my favorites, in a corporate news release from a Saskatchewan chemical company: "The project will lead to the commercial development of a granular innoculant which will enhance the uptake of nitrogen in legume crops."

Enhance the uptake?? Why not just spit it out -- they're making fertilizer, for crying out loud.

The all-time worst offender I've ever encountered, though, was the Transport Canada official explaining a near-collision in the skies over Calgary last month: "There was a loss of separation between the two aircraft."

A loss of separation??? Boy, talk about trying to cast in a positive light.

There should be a law against this vocabulary abuse. Something along the lines of Attempting to Obstruct the Passage of Information. Deliberate and Willful Linguistic Misconduct. Erection of Artificial and Unauthorized Language Barriers.

It should be a Capital Offence.

COMMAS -- THE PAUSE THAT REFRESHES

On the wall in the production facility in Banff from whence this tiny tabloid is issued each Monday hangs a copy of a headline that once adorned a Dave Barry column. It reads: *Editing Kills Four Million Brain Cells Each Year.*

I can relate.

To be on a never-ending search for misspelled words, improperly used adverbs, unattributed quotations or the innovative phrases of the homonym-challenged reporter who will "peak" your curiosity or allow fires to "raise" houses to the ground was not what I had planned to be when I grew up.

(I'm still, to this day, not sure just what it was I aspired to, but finding and correcting the participle that dares dangle was not what I would have figured was a fun way to make a living.)

Editors are among the most obsessive individuals known to mankind. They edit everything -- junk mail, letters from friends, road signs with misplaced apostrophes, menus, tombstones, anything on which the printed word is displayed. Mistakes drive us nuts, and our greatest glee is experienced when we find something written by a teacher -- *especially* an English teacher -- that contains even the most innocuous of mistakes.

Each week I get to sift trough mounds of material submitted by both hired writers and unpaid correspondents, and each week I am struck anew by the *laissez faire* attitude our society exhibits toward punctuation, particularly the comma.

There seems to be a general perception in the world that commas are something totally unrelated to the act of writing and are to be used at whim, sprinkled liberally throughout one's writing like so much confetti at a wedding.

I once worked with a reporter who had to be put on a weekly "comma quota", so indiscriminately did he pepper his prose with subordinate clauses.

Then there was the reporter who never used them, and upon being told that one should usually insert a comma each time one paused in reading, insisted that, as a non-smoker, he had less cause to pause.

Most people would find this obsession with punctuation a trifle excessive and say hey, what does it matter where the comma goes? People know what I'm trying to say, right? Well...maybe.

I am reminded of all of this by a column I recently read in the Canadian Community Newspaper Association's *Publisher* magazine, which related the tale of a ruler who had received a message asking whether a prisoner was to be pardoned or put to death.

The message was: "Execute him not to be freed."

The jailers read the message by could make no sense of it, until one realized a comma was missing. He placed it after the word "not", and the prisoner was set free. The ruler was furious, however, because the comma should have been placed after the word "him".

Literally a life or death issue, you could say -- a classic case of punctuate or perish.

HEY MARTHA! DID YOU
HEAR THE ONE ABOUT

February 16, 1993

Something unusual happened at my house last week. We changed the channel.

(Throughout this seasonal football and baseball drought, TSN still has many, many exciting options for your viewing enjoyment, in addition to the 1,575 weekly hockey games which we've come to love and expect. There's paraplegic tennis, for example. Five-pin bowling, live from Sudbury. Or, my personal favorite, Saturday morning interviews with 12-year-old skateboard prodigies about their favorite abandoned culverts.)

We changed the channel to watch Oprah interview Michael. And who didn't? Exists there a soul in this town who doesn't now know Michael only admits to two cosmetic alterations and is turning white because he has a skin disorder? Exists there a soul who believes it? (This is a rhetorical question. Please, no unsolicited manuscripts to the Editor.)

Michael and his modifications are the kind of story known in the cannibalistic news biz as a "Hey Martha!" The origin of this particular journalistic jargon is somewhat obscure, but it goes something like this:

Somewhere in middle America sits a man, reading his evening paper or watching TV while his wife Martha is in the kitchen fixing dinner. When he comes across the story about space aliens conducting unauthorized neurosurgery or corpses found in the boxsprings of none-too-clean Edmonton hotel rooms he shouts: "Hey *Martha!* Listen to *this!*"

Or so they say. I have no idea from whence this sexist tale originated or whether there ever was a Martha, but every reporter in the world knows about Mr. Martha and his susceptibility to outlandish news stories. Mr. Martha is why tabloids flourish and Oprah Winfrey gets exclusive

Michael Jackson interviews that are necessary to refute all the other Hey Marthas! the tabs have printed about him.

And now perfectly serious news reporters are running around interviewing doctors to see if it's possible that Michael *really does* have some exotic skin disorder and whether it will now be known as the Michael Jackson blotch.

Hey Marthas! are kind of the media version of "Nyaa! Nyaa! Made you look! Made you look!"

Are Hey Marthas! news? Of course. Not the kind of news that collapses governments and deposes despots (although Imelda Marcos' shoe closet was a definite Hey Martha!) but the kind of news that makes everyone sit up and take notice. Kind of like real good gossip, weird little snippets of life that are almost so bizarre you can't imagine making anything like that up.

How many of your started your Monday morning coffee breaks with "Hey, did you hear about the body in the box- spring... ?" Thought so.

Unfortunately, in Canmore Hey Marthas! are a little hard to come by. I'm not sure if off-sales in Exshaw and publicly-shorn elected officials qualify, and when last we checked there were no bodies in the local boxsprings. Lots of bodies in beds where they don't belong, but thus far we've resisted community pressure to report on those. (Definitely Hey Marthas! though.)

CANADIANS NEED A NATIONAL MULLIGAN DAY

August 10, 1993

A couple of weeks ago, a local resident making a presentation to Council maligned the game of golf as environmentally unfriendly, elitist, decadent and boring. (Sounds like the provincial cabinet, doesn't it?)

It may be true. Then again, it may not. (Note the carefully worded refusal to take sides. In my two years as captain of this little paper boat, I have learned one lesson extremely well. Never stake out a position on an issue that has the potential to alienate you from at least 50 per cent of the population, regardless of which side you support. Sit on the fence and agree with both, yessirree.)

I do want to raise one point in defence of golf, however, and praise that single, sterling, redeeming quality that if applied to life as we know it would make this world a far better place.

Mulligans. For all you non-partakers of the sport, a Mulligan is a chance to reload and take another shot from the tee box if your drive goes into the woods, the water or the magnetic railway tracks on the third fairway.

(Serious golfers who actually keep track of their handicaps never take Mulligans, of course, but personally I think not being a permitted Mulligan user is a handicap unto itself.)

Believe it or not, Mulligans are a purely Canadian invention with a surprising Canmore connection. The term was apparently coined in the late 1920s in Montreal where, it seems, the only owner of a car among a dedicated four-some was one Irishman named David Mulligan, whose arms and hands were so badly rattled after the weekly 50 kilometer drive to the St. Lambert Country Club over potholes and cross-ties that the other members of his group allowed him a second drive from the first tee. Hence the term "taking a Mulligan." (Mr. Mulligan was allegedly the cousin of Coun-cillor Terry Wall's mother, and if you doubt the veracity of this tale take it up with him, not me.)

Wouldn't you just love to take a Mulligan on life sometimes, when confronted with God's little sand traps?

You know those mornings when you get out of bed and your hair is molded into the shape of Mount Rundle and the imprint of a blanket fold is fused into your cheekbone and you have 37 seconds to get to work? Wouldn't it be nice to take a Mulligan, go back to bed and try again tomorrow?

How about in those truly disastrous social situations, where you hear yourself expounding to a total stranger about the tackiness of black leatherette wet bars just as you spot one in the corner and realize the stranger is your host? Take a Mulligan. Expunge the record and start again.

Caught in a speed trap? Excuse me officer, can I take a Mulligan on that?

Inadvertently call your new boyfriend by your old boyfriend's name? Mulligan time. Bounce a cheque at the bank? Oops. Take a Mulligan and try again.

The possibilities are limitless. Our politicians really should recognize this Canadian contribution to the game of golf and declare a National Mulligan Day. They of all people should recognize its advantages.

WOULD YOU EAT PUDDING FROM A TIN?

April 6, 1993

I'm starting to get the feeling that we as a society no longer have our collective heads screwed on straight.

Why did scientists spend all that time and money learning how to take the color out of a soft drink and why are we buying it? Didn't know you couldn't live without it, did you?

We now have clear beer and colorized movies. Correct me if I'm wrong, but I really don't think the world was holding its breath for these earth-shattering developments. Accurate weather predictions, maybe. A cure for cancer, definitely. But colorless intoxicants? They've never been particularly high on *my* list of must-haves.

Neither were glow-in-the-dark toothbrushes. Science has now made it possible for me to get up in the middle of the night and see the instrument I am using to remove from my teeth that which I could not actually see when it passed my lips.

The list of new discoveries from the research labs has gone from the sublime to the ridiculous. Jalapeno potato chips. Microwave popcorn. Kleenex with lotion. Sanitary napkins with wings.

(Well, okay, that last one was pretty good. So were snooze buttons. And Velcro, a truly brilliant concept that allows women to actually *rip* the shoulder pads out of their dresses without damaging the fabric.)

Highlighter pens. Now I ask you, how much more efficient are we now that we no longer have to underline? Do these things actually contribute significantly to our betterment as a society, and how much money did the guy who invented them get paid?

Don't even *bother* to ask me how I feel about air pumps for running shoes and bikini tops.

Sometimes it seems that science is out of control. As an industry it has spent entirely too much effort coming up with products that are mindboggling in their uselessness and questionable in their safety -- and not just the really horrible bad inventions, like nuclear waste. We're talking stupid bad, like pudding in a tin. And instant tea, for those among us so truly lazy they can't expend the energy to dunk a teabag.

Now our politicians are talking about the need to spend more on research and development, no doubt fearing we're falling behind in the race to build a better home karaoke machine so the world will beat a path to our door.

We're caught in a vicious cycle, sold on the premise that these new gadgets will make our lives easier and allow us more time to play. Then we're sold more gadgets so we'll have something to do with all this alleged increased leisure time, but most of us are too busy working to pay for all these new toys and food facsimiles we didn't know we needed.

Personally I think it's the scientists these days that have altogether too much time on their hands. All they're *really* looking for is new places for us to park our money.

AND YOU THOUGH
THE TWILIGHT ZONE WAS A MYTH

February 22, 1994

The world of late night advertising is a weird and wondrous place.

It's a virtual cornucopia for the horizontally inclined of a certain target age group. The worker bee adults are assumed to be asleep, the adolescents more importantly occupied and the infants uninterested. The only people still alert in television land are assumed to be retired, semi-retired or wishing they were so.

How else can one explain the abundance of retro-rock collections of the Greatest Hits of the '50s, on vinyl no less? Who else would they be aimed at than insomniac baby boomers sitting up in their rocking chairs, awaiting their semi-grown offspring to hit curfew? Rocking around the clock, as it were.

Adjustable beds and noise-activated light switches. Bunion cures and arthritis antidotes and teeth whiteners and house/car/garage alarm systems. This is our life, fellow aged ones, infirmity and fear. Yellow teeth and stiff joints.

Adult diapers have entered our collective conscious-ness. Weak kidneys, this is what we have to look forward to. Why are they not flogged like Pampers, I wonder, with one style for the boys and another for the girls? Is it only women who have bladder control problems? Apparently so, just as it's evident only women have those embarrassing little itch-ing problems. Sexism follows us all the days of our lives.

Gelatinous hair dye for beards and mustaches. Hair replacement tonics and self-adhesive toupees. Vanity, thy name is man.

Stair masters and thigh-shrinking creams and simu-lated nordic ski tracks. Exercise equipment for those so truly tied to the cathode ray that they would rather spend $200 so they can work up a sweat to the *Jeopardy* theme than go outside and be exposed to real life.

In the wee, tiny hours, when the Hubble is scanning the heavens for fractured comets, our antennae pick up messages from society's parasites, yesteryear's snake oil salesmen flogging their get-rich-quick-by-contributing-absolutely-nothing-worthwhile-to-this-planet schemes. Get yourself a 1-900 number, hire a couple of women with breathless voices and you're in business. Party Line. Date Line. Chat Line. Desperate For The Sound Of Another Human Voice Line. Only $5 a minute, all of it yours.

Too complicated? Try mass advertising in the classifieds. Offer something totally worthless for sale, spend a few dollars a week in a few thousand papers and watch the bucks pour in. *Your lifetime horoscope. Psychic Masters... True love and happiness can be yours... send $19.95... Professional writers help you find fame and fortune... send $39.95 now for 16-week lesson plan...*

Half-hour infomercials on wise investing. Playing the market. Buying insurance. Choosing stocks. When to buy and when to sell. Freedom 55 is now our favorite fantasy. We are consumed by money -- how to get it, how to save it, how to spend it, how to hoard it.

All in all, it's a pretty depressing scenario. Money and Age. The two are inextricably linked. If you're advancing in the latter, you'd better have lots of the former.

Actually, what's really depressing is that I seem to be their perfect target viewing audience, because that's when they choose to show *Get Smart* and *The Twilight Zone* and *The Man From U.N.C.L.E.* What this says about me, I prefer not to think about.

FINDING A GLOBAL CURE
FOR MORNING SICKNESS

June 23, 1992

Have you heard the one about Carlos, the Pregnant Man of the Phillipines?

Yes, it's true. (Well, actually, it's not, but read on.)

A few weeks back Carlos made international headlines by claiming to be a six-months' pregnant hermaphrodite, born with both male and female sex organs. Later in life, after having some body parts lopped, he'd been transformed into a woman and soon thereafter found herself pregnant. Man-woman-child, all in one body. Your ultimate, nuclear family kind of guy.

But just when the story was getting *really* interesting and doctors were publicly speculating on the logistics of the delivery, it all turned out to be a hoax. Old Carlos was just pulling our collective leg. He was a man, albeit a troubled man, but just a man all the same, looking for a little global attention.

Still, the news did cause a few eyebrows to raise, including those of yours truly. Not so much at the perversity of the whole yarn, but at the concept.

If men could have babies...

If men could have babies, an effective, safe, absolutely-guaranteed, no side effects birth control would be on the market in about 10 nanoseconds. The price of condoms would plummet.

A pill would be found that was 100 per cent effective, without fear of strokes, heart attacks, high blood pressure, mood alterations, water retention or additional facial hair. (Although, they could probably develop and market the latter for those guys who wanted a more macho appearance while fending off unwanted paternity.)

If men could have babies, kazillions of medical research dollars would be siphoned from international defence budgets in a global race to find a cure for morning sickness.

Work contracts would be rewritten to guarantee three months of sick leave at the outset of any pregnancy to accommodate this, and paternity leave would be enshrined in the constitution for no less than one year following the birth of one's child to allow sufficient time to recover from pain and suffering.

Prospective nannies would leapfrog to the head of every immigration queue and day care workers would find themselves in the same wage bracket as hockey announcers and auto mechanics. Corporations would miraculously see the need for on-site day care in every place of employment as more and more of their bright young boys started phoning in sick because the sitter didn't show up.

Abortion, of course, would not only cease to be an issue but would be covered by Medicare and fully insured in most benefits package.

Magazines would start sprouting features on *Restoring Those Post-Natal Pecs* and *Will The Baby Bulge Bother Your Backswing?* The term Paternity Suit would take on a whole new meaning, with elasticized pinstriped trousers for that expanding waistline.

Wild oats would no doubt be saved, not sown, once the onus of harvesting them fell equally upon the male shoulder, and the term "singe dad" would *never* become synonymous with irresponsible, promiscuous, morally questionable or welfare cheat.

None of this, of course, will ever happen. Old Carlos was merely raising false hopes. But it does make for a fond fantasy, the notion of making the consequences of one's actions such a fearsome personal threat that the word "responsibility" would actually factor into the decision.

A SIMPLE SOLUTION TO
A SLIGHT IMBALANCE

July 21, 1992

Police Barely Able to Cope. Rally Falls Flat. Perky Protesters Imprisoned. Nipples Nixed. Boobs Banned. Bosoms Heaved.

Headline writers across Canada could have had a field day with this one, but it would seem the nation's first topless protest rally was somewhat of a bust.

In some places, shirtless men showed up en masse to support women who want the same right to go topless in public. The women were arrested and hustled from view. In other places, women kept their shirts on when faced with hundreds of less than supportive men looking for a free peep show.

Women are paid to bare their breasts on a stage in a dark, smoky bar, but on a hot sunny day in a public park it's against the law. It's considered sport to dump buckets of cold water on women so their nipples stand out under their T-shirts, but take away that flimsy material and she's under arrest. Magazines showing women's airbrushed chests are openly displayed on magazine racks at eye level but it's illegal to see the real, imperfect thing on the beach.

Even the woman who sparked the protest with her conviction for taking off her shirt on a hot July day last year, Gwen Jacob, opted to disrobe in the U.S. where seven women in New York recently had their convictions for going topless overturned. It's illegal in Canada, but not in the U.S.?

The problem is, we breast owners don't know what to think anymore. We're confused. We live in an imperfect world of double and changing standards. Different body parts are considered sexually desirable by the geographical luck of the draw. In some parts of Africa, women are sexy if they have huge thighs and buttocks (although you don't see a thriving industry over there to inject potentially carcinogenic substances in their butts to make them bigger, but that's another issue). In Japan, the nape of the neck is ostensibly the most desired spot. In North America, it's huge breasts, but it hasn't always been this way. In the flapper era of the 1920s women bound their breasts tightly to their chests, and in the 1960s Twiggy made it fashionable once more to be less than ample. In between and since, there's been Jayne Mansfield, Jane Russell, Marilyn Monroe and Dolly Parton.

One Calgary newspaper runs full-color photos of bikini-clad women on page three every day and the other gets a flood of protest letters when they refer to Billy Ray Cyrus' cute butt.

The scales of justice and moral equality are a little unbalanced. Why are breasts supposed to be covered and who said so? Were women consulted in this? Did the person who invented the bra ever ask women if they really felt this was necessary?

Personally, I think that instead of baring our boobs in public we should be fighting to force men to cover up those parts of *their* bodies that *we* find tempting. Fair's fair. If we have to cover ours, they should have to cover theirs.

Some women would insist on men covering their legs. Some would vote for chests, hairy or otherwise. A few I know would say it's the hands.

To me, the sexiest part of a man's body is his eyes. I think all men should be forced to cover their eyes when in public.

Wait a minute...

ANGST IS ONLY IN THE
EYE OF THE BEHOLDER

August 3, 1992

Recently a male friend of mine pointed out that an article in this month's *Flare* magazine about women and their supposed lack of assertiveness described at least half the men he knew.

Can't be, said I. Obviously that's a special woman-type problem, because it's in a special, woman-type magazine. (Besides, you guys have enough problems of your own, you can't have ours, too -- unless you want to take this little water retention dilemma off our hands. That you can have.) One of our biggest problems, to my way of thinking, is this multi-kazillion dollar publishing industry that's geared toward proving that women are all riddled with angst over things like eyebrow stubble and outdated china patterns, then professing to offer help so we can solve these earth-shattering crises and sleep more easily on our hand-embroidered percale pillowcases.

The headlines on these glossies give one the impression that we are focused only on sex, food and dieting, finding a man, keeping a man and then weaning him of all his annoying little habits. (Although I've yet to see any really practical advice, like how to keep him from immediately switching channels to TSN to catch the highlights of the game he's just finished watching on CBC.)

According to some of the best sellers on the newsstands this month, we women fret about our children growing up to be serial killers and our parents moving to town to be closer to the homicidal grandchildren. We are consumed with guilt over having made and eaten the chocolate torte on page 16 so now we must turn to page 39 to learn Quick and Easy Steps to Leaner Legs.

We are all desperate to know painless hair removal techniques while at the same time we hunger to know how to drape our bodies from shoulder to ankle in multiple layers of rags for the chic bag lady look that's de rigueur for fall fashion. (Just why is it women have to know how to layer and men don't, anyway?)

And if your decorating budget is tight, there's even step-by-step directions for creating wonderful window dressings with flowered bed sheets. (Now, if I started decorating our windows with flowered sheets my partner would likely insist on separate residences, but according to these magazines he secretly harbors an intense desire to have me imprint my feminine touch on our shared domicile. And all this time I thought I'd already done that by leaving my tampons in the cabinet under the bathroom sink.)

Every month at least one of these publications offers a questionnaire on such tripe as: "Are you truly right for each other?" or "How well do you *really* know your mate?" in which you're both supposed to answer the questions and then compare responses.

("Of *course* I love you darling, but first tell me, what are the three most important items in your wallet right now and as a child, did you feel secure, neglected or geeky?")

We may have our first woman Prime Minister, but I don't think we'll be truly equal until we see features like *How to Have a Hassle Free Holiday with the Kids* on the front cover of *Men's Journal*.

GOOD GRIEF MURPHY BROWN!
WHAT NEXT?

May 26, 1992

The biggest news story this past week was, of course, the revelation that dinosaurs are not extinct. They have merely evolved, ever so slightly, into American vice-presidents.

The Cold War is over, the Gulf War is over, Noriega's behind bars and Dan Quayle feels a little left out of the primaries. What's left? Murphy Brown's single motherhood.

Here's a fictional single woman of the '90s who, if we're to believe a man whose golf score outweighs his IQ, has single-handedly lowered the morals and values of American society by having a baby. (Well, maybe not single-handedly. There *was* that good looking ex-husband who skipped town at the beginning of the season after doing the dirty deed, but guys don't seem to figure much in this little controversy. Dan's not upset with ex-husbands who flee responsibility, only with the women who take it.)

There have been other single moms on TV before, on shows like *Alice* and *One Day at a Time*, but they don't count. They were divorced. They at one time had husbands and (we assume) did the right thing and married before having sex. They were single moms by circumstance, which is okay, rather than by choice, which is not.

There have been other characters on TV who have had sex outside of marriage. Lots of them. Lots and lots and lots of them. On pretty much every show on every channel at any time of the day. On beer commercials, even.

Sam Malone can chase every skirt that comes into his bar and get lucky with half of them, but does Quayle object to *that* depreciating the morals and values of the American viewing public? Nope. Ditto for Dan Fielding.

Women can do it too, as long as they have absolutely infallible birth control which, judging by the amount of sex and lack of babies being produced, Hollywood has but refuses to share with the rest of the world.

Murphy must have forgotten to get some from the prop room.

Dan Quayle doesn't object to sex *per se* -- remember, this is the guy who bought that obscene little phallic doll down in Samoa to take home because he thought it was "neat". He just objects to women who have sex and get pregnant without benefit of clergy.

Nancy Reagan, of course, doesn't count. As soon as she found out she was in the family way she got old Ronnie to divorce Jane and hustle her down the aisle just as quick as could be. No illegitimacy in that family, nope.

Murphy should've Just Said No when that good looking charmer whatsisname hit down back in September. Then she wouldn't have found herself in this whole mess.

But when faced with the consequences Murphy chose to do what Bush and Quayle would have wanted. She chose not to have an abortion.

There's only one logical step left to her now that would appease Mr. Quayle and his party's line. Give the baby up for adoption to a loving home, with two parents, where it will receive the kind of upbringing every child deserves and the benefit of both mother and father's influence.

Maybe to someone like Al and Peg Bundy. At least they're married.

FINDING JOY IN THE
LITTLE THINGS IN LIFE

January 5, 1993

As 1992 drew to a close last week, political pundits across North America got out their 20/20 rear view mirrors and declared it The Worst Year That Ever Was.

Page upon page of newsprint was filled with bloated, morose analysis pieces bemoaning the referendum (and how all those obstinate voters refused to listen to the media on which way to vote); the economy (and how it was affecting Southam, TorStar and the CBC and may actually mean their own overpaid punditry positions are endangered); the growing number of homeless people; the rise of neo-Nazism; famine in Somalia; celebrity heterosexual AIDS victims and the inclusion of *Sex!* (gasp!) in public libraries.

Okay, okay, in some ways things weren't that great. But it really wasn't *that* bad. We're just not looking hard enough for that old silver lining. Personally, I think 1992 was one of the best years we've ever seen because

1. Don Getty not only resigned, he *volunteered* to stay out of the Legislature for the next year *and* pay his own rent while he sifts through seven years' of correspondence and decides what to burn. What a guy!

2. A cat's family was elected to the White House and its owner, unlike his canine fraternizing predecessors, lost no time in issuing a sternly worded edict to the press -- Don't Touch The Cat. The U.S. finally elected a president with his head on straight. He didn't pick Socks up by the

ears to provide a better photo-op and he probably won't let it write a book, either.

3. We finally got proof positive, courtesy of the venerable poller of the community Angus Reid, that men spend as much time in the bathroom as women. End of argument.

4. The Blue Jays won and the U.S. now knows what a Canadian flag looks like right side up. Fourteen million American adolescents are now guaranteed to get at least one question right on their next geography exam.

5. Mike Tyson went to jail and Superman died -- both role models for little boys throughout North America and both obscene distortions of what little boys should aspire to.

6. Curling became a competitive, money-making, TSN-recognized sport, one of only two known to mankind where age, weight and sex are irrelevant and an ability to break a sweat is not requisite. Gotta love those Scots.

7. The prototype of the world's first self-parking car was unveiled in New York City, and while it's still probably decades away from mass production, we have cause for hope.

8. The Miss Canada pageant died after decades of trying to convince little girls they wanted to grow up to be the kind of women Mike Tyson would be attracted to.

9. We learned that Princess Diana, probably *the* most artificially poised and polished woman ever placed before a camera, goes by the nickname Squidgey in her more intimate moments. Shorties, Tubbies, Lumpies and Porkys the world over rejoiced. Her sister-in-law did equally well in raising the international sex appeal quotient of toe-sucking bald men.

10. The NovAtel boondoggle *only* cost us $566.6 million. It could have been worse.

MAKING PROMISES I KNOW I CAN KEEP

December 29, 1992

Two days from now, thousands of otherwise, intelligent people are going to indulge in a centuries-old tradition that will see them wake up with the dawn of a New Year wondering what demon possessed them the night before.

Not the demon rum, although that may have had a good hold on them. No, we're talking about the demon that paves the road to hell. The demon of Good Intentions, the force which at this time of year inspires most of us to make public statements of pending failure.

These are called New Year's Resolutions, and they are the reason you asked for and received a Thighmaster for Christmas. On Friday you are going to use that Thighmaster. Maybe even Saturday. By May it will be advertised for sale in the classified ads of this very paper. Or in the garbage with your nicotine patches.

Has anybody out there actually kept a New Year's Resolution? Tossed your cigarettes and lighter out the back door at the stroke of midnight and *not* gone in search of them the next morning? Enrolled in a correspondence course and actually finished the work? Anybody out there even marginally skinnier/wealthier/smarter or a better cook than at this time last year?

Right.

Personally, I have never made a New Year's Resolution I could not keep. This is nothing much to be proud of, because from one year to the next I am not a significantly better person. I just don't see any percentage in setting unrealistic goals. I only make promises to which I know I can faithfully adhere.

This year, for example, I promise to keep smoking, drinking and staying up too late.

I will not lose weight. I might even gain some. My advancing age may redistribute some of it, but no one will notice and if they do I will ignore them.

I will continue to save money toward the downpayment on a house in my usual, methodical fashion. Pennies in a jar. I will continue to raid that jar when I run out of cigarettes the day before payday.

I promise to make at least half of you good readers irate with every editorial I write, and I will continue to be my unfailingly polite self when you phone to tell me in your usually diplomatic way that I am full of bull.

I will continue to put mistakes in the *Canmore Leader,* just for those of you whose chief source of amusement in life seems to be finding those mistakes and pointing them out to me. In that same vein, I promise I will never again refer to Doug Flutie as the Calgary Flames quarterback.

I will wash my car at least once this year, probably in the spring. I may even give it a tune up, but that's not a promise.

I will continue to support the Marigold Library System with hefty infusions of cash in lieu of returning my books on time.

I will heed the fashion gods and update my wardrobe with at least one new sweatshirt this year. It will not have a sports logo on it.

And I will continue to shop locally, or at least until they declare a Rural Drivers Only Day in Calgary.